The Life
Behind the
Voice

M. R.
DeHaan

Founder of Radio Bible Class,
home of *Our Daily Bread*

The Life
Behind the
Voice

M. R. DeHaan

Founder of Radio Bible Class,
home of *Our Daily Bread*

JAMES R. ADAIR

DISCOVERY HOUSE
PUBLISHERS®

Feeding the Soul with the Word of God

This is an expanded, updated version of *M. R. De Haan—The Man and His Ministry,* © 1969 by Zondervan Publishing House, Grand Rapids, Michigan.

Discovery House Publishers is affiliated with RBC Ministries, Grand Rapids, Michigan.

Discovery House books are distributed to the trade exclusively by Barbour Publishing, Inc., Uhrichsville, Ohio.

Requests for permission to quote from this book should be directed to Permissions Department, Discovery House Publishers, P.O. Box 3566, Grand Rapids, MI 49501.

Scripture quotations are from the King James Version, unless otherwise indicated.

Library of Congress Cataloging-in-Publication Data available on request.

Interior design by Nicholas Richardson

Printed in the United States of America

08 09 10 11 12 13 / BPI / 10 9 8 7 6 5 4 3 2 1

To the memory of
Priscilla DeHaan,
whose graces, as M. R. DeHaan stated
in the dedication of his first book,
reminded him daily of the reality of the power
of the Word in Christian life.

CONTENTS

FOREWORD

Just outside my office hangs a remarkable likeness of my grandfather, M. R. DeHaan.* The unnerving thing about this portrait is that it is hung in such a way that when I step outside my office, the Doctor seems to be looking right at me. Fortunately, the twinkle in his eye and the half smile on his face look exactly as I remember him.

Any decorator would tell you that the picture is much too large for the wall on which it hangs. It's the kind of portrait that should be hung in a large room with big walls and a high ceiling. But, while we have no intention of enshrining our founder, it seems appropriate to have this oversized portrait reminding my co-workers and me of what we believe God did with a life given back to Him.

As the pages of my grandfather's story will show, he was a down-to-earth and ordinary man who shared with his grandchildren a love for gardening, laughter, and fishing for bass on a quiet lake. More important, he gave us an example of a man deeply committed to the Bible, to the good news of grace, and to the anticipation of the any-moment return of Christ.

---

* This portrait was painted by Dan Richardson, founder of Florida's WAYRadio and sent as a gift to us after Dan's passing. You can see the portrait at the WAYRadio Web site http://am.wayradio.org/history.php.

Because, in the providence of God, the influence of M. R. DeHaan went far beyond his family, I am pleased that we are able to offer this updated edition of his biography on the 70th anniversary of the Bible-teaching outreach he founded.

MART DEHAAN
President, RBC Ministries
Grand Rapids, Michigan
June, 2008

Foreword to the First Edition

A book such as this would never have been written had my father been the one to make the decision. During his entire ministry he said little concerning his own life, and minimized the things others said about him, which seemed to him to be self-glory.

Now that he has gone "Home" and his labors have ended, however, it is most fitting and proper that this volume be published, not to magnify a man, but to glorify God and to demonstrate what He can do through one who makes himself available.

God does accomplish His work through His children. He could have chosen special heavenly emissaries, but in supreme wisdom God made the very ones who have experienced His saving grace to be the channels through which the glorious news of redemption should be communicated. As in past ages chosen human vessels conveyed God's message, so today the Lord raises up men to speak to their generation. Such was John the Baptist, of whom the Bible says, "There was a *man* sent from God . . ." (John 1:6). My father also was a divinely appointed messenger, and in this biography you will see God at work through a *man*—one just as human as you or I, and subject to the same limitations and frailties. To recognize that the

Lord uses human instruments in the fulfillment of His divine program should be an encouragement to every believer.

The memories I have of my father are precious. He was a man strong in spirit, with deep, uncompromising convictions. I can recall hearing him say, "I don't care if the *whole world* is against me, I must stand for what I believe is right." Yet, although firm and steadfast, he was known by his associates to be an unusually warm-hearted person, having an earnest compassion for others and a genuine love for his Lord. These are qualities that I would seek to emulate.

His faithful teaching of the Word of God, however, has made the greatest impression upon my life. When he was led into the ministry and turned his back on the practice of medicine, which he loved, this new and higher calling became his all-consuming passion. And God honored his dedication.

I pray, as this volume is sent forth, that the life and ministry of my father will be used to lead many, especially the young in years, to take a firm stand upon the Word of God, and to make themselves available in His hands to do His bidding. God has His men for every generation. If just one should read these pages and through them be aroused into active service, then the "making of this book" shall not have been in vain. Rather, it will be another chapter in the ongoing ministry of M. R. DeHaan, M.D., a "man sent from God," who, "being dead, yet speaketh." Then even he would approve of this work, for he could say with the great apostle, "they praised God because of me" (Galatians 1:24).

RICHARD W. DeHAAN, 1969
Grand Rapids, Michigan

ABOUT THIS BOOK

So far as I could determine, Dr. M. R. DeHaan never told his fascinating story publicly—certainly not in detail. He didn't want the spotlight turned on him. His God-given message was what mattered, he often said.

I learned his attitude firsthand in 1964 when I approached him following a church service and suggested a biographical article for *Power for Living*, a weekly publication of which I was then editor, but he wasn't interested. Then, in 1965, after Dr. DeHaan's death, Radio Bible Class officials decided that the DeHaan story should be put in permanent form to show how the power of God worked through a life. I was pleased when Zondervan Publishing House, unaware of my earlier interest in Dr. DeHaan's story, asked me to write this biography for Radio Bible Class.

As I conducted numerous interviews and pored over clippings and other published material, I discovered Dr. DeHaan was indeed the colorful, godly person I had assumed him to be. Known to most listeners of *Radio Bible Class* only as a beloved, gravelly-voiced teacher, he was a man of great drive and brilliance, a leader of unusual spiritual depth and insight, a disciple as human as Simon Peter.

I am indebted to many people who willingly shared information and insights, including members of the DeHaan family, the Radio Bible Class staff, longtime friends of Dr. DeHaan, and others.

This updated and expanded volume does not pretend to deal in depth with all of the facets of Dr. DeHaan's life, but mainly with those events and facts that the late Richard DeHaan and other Radio Bible Class officials believed would be of special interest and value to "Class members" and others who have followed the DeHaan ministry. According to Richard, his father's successor in the radio ministry, "The entire story would fill volumes. In this biography on my father and his ministry, we hope to show how God led step by step in achieving His purpose."

JAMES R. ADAIR
Wheaton, Illinois

THE M. R. DEHAAN FAMILY

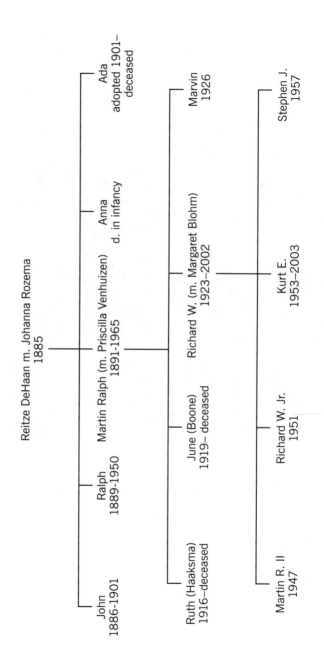

Reitze DeHaan m. Johanna Rozema
1885

John
1886-1901

Ralph
1889-1950

Martin Ralph (m. Priscilla Venhuizen)
1891-1965

Anna
d. in infancy

Ada
adopted 1901–
deceased

Ruth (Haaksma)
1916–deceased

June (Boone)
1919– deceased

Richard W. (m. Margaret Blohm)
1923–2002

Marvin
1926

Martin R. II
1947

Richard W. Jr.
1951

Kurt E.
1953–2003

Stephen J.
1957

CHAPTER 1

BOY AT A STREET MEETING

"I have lent him to the Lord; as long as he liveth he shall be lent to the Lord. . . ."

I SAMUEL 1:28

A smile played at the corners of her thin, stern mouth and tears of joy welled in her blue eyes that warm morning of June 11, 1901, as Johanna DeHaan watched fifteen-year-old John, her eldest son, leave for school. To her, there was no finer lad in the town of Zeeland, Michigan, nor elsewhere throughout the surrounding Dutch colony. She dabbed her eyes with her white apron, taking care that her younger sons, Ralph and Martin, didn't see her and misunderstand her tears.

From a window of the two-story red brick home on the corner of Lincoln and Peck Streets, Johanna, a plumpish woman of thirty-five, watched her son disappear on his way toward Zeeland High School on Main Street. Then she returned to her kitchen chores, remembering last night's discussion with her husband.

"Reitze, it's time we made some decision regarding John's further schooling. He's finishing ninth grade, and it's not too early for us to start planning how we'll send him to college."

Reitze DeHaan was the town cobbler, a gentle, practical man who wanted the best for his family, though most of the time he made not much more than a dollar a day, hardly enough to assure each of his children a college education.

Johanna, who most certainly had more than an equal vote in family decisions, suggested they should tighten up even more on their spending and begin looking into the matter of a loan for John's advanced schooling, likely at Hope College in nearby Holland, Michigan.

By the light of a kerosene lamp, the DeHaans talked of the professions and occupations that John might study for: businessman, lawyer, doctor, preacher. . . . Of course, only John himself, who had not yet said what he wanted to be, could really decide, they concluded. "How nice it would be if God called him to be a minister," mused Johanna. Reitze agreed that this would be the fulfillment of their dreams and prayers.

Before school that Tuesday morning, June 11, Johanna had shared with John the news that they were definitely planning to send him to college.

John's face brightened and he looked past his mother out the window as if trying to penetrate the future. "Let's see, I'm fifteen now, and by the time I'm twenty-two, the Lord willing, I will be a minister."

These words sent an electric tingle down Johanna's spine, and she pondered them as John rode his bike toward Zeeland High.

That afternoon, following school, John and a friend, Herman Boone, rode their bikes to a lake-like stretch of the Black River west of Zeeland called Boone's River. With other school friends, they gathered water lilies for botany class. The fun was over and the others were starting home when John and Herman called,

"There are some nicer lilies out there; we're going to stay and get them. We'll catch up with you on our bikes."

What happened after that was never fully known. Harry and Thomas Vander Pels, of Zeeland, who were fishing, saw the two boys picking water lilies about 4:45 that afternoon. As they left to fish farther upstream, the two boys were stripping for a swim. Then about 6:30 the two men returned to the spot where the boys had been and noticed their clothes on the riverbank, but the boys were nowhere in sight. Afraid that the boys might have drowned, the fishermen began raking the bottom of the river with their cane poles. Within fifteen minutes they discovered the boys' bodies in about six feet of water and about six feet apart.

❋   ❋   ❋

For Johanna and Reitze DeHaan, the dream of having their eldest son become a minister had been shattered within a few hours. The gentle, shimmering Black River had become a slithering, greedy monster, snuffing out the lives of the two teenagers. And John's last words to his mother, which had thrilled Johanna's heart, were to linger only as memories and suggest what might have been.

While young John had enjoyed attending church services with his family at the First Christian Reformed Church in Zeeland and had taken his catechism classes seriously, neither his brother Ralph, the next oldest, nor the youngest, Martin, showed the inclinations that John had exhibited. Eleven-year-old Ralph also gave himself seriously to things of the church, but he was quiet and somewhat of an introvert. Ten-year-old Martin, on the other hand, was more of an extrovert and an earthy kind of lad who was more interested in Crackerjacks (and the prize inside the box), frogs, pollywogs, and skunks—and following the town lamplighter from corner to corner in the evening.

Once, when Reitze asked a visiting minister to offer thanks for the food at the dinner table, Martin had embarrassed his parents by saying, "Could you please make it short, so we can get on with the meal?"

But there came a day when, at least to Martin, it seemed that God's hand had touched him in a special way.

❊   ❊   ❊

Periodically the slow clop, clop of horses' hooves and the creaking of a buckboard wagon moving into town from the west, carrying a tall woman evangelist, drew swarms of young Hollanders to Main Street in Zeeland. Dressed in wide-collared shirts, short corduroy pants or knickers, long stockings and high-top shoes, the youngsters scampered from their white frame and red brick houses with steep gabled roofs and skinny windows to taunt the woman with the thundering voice who preached from the buckboard. Her name was Nellie Churchford, and she came from the City Mission in Holland. She was a sort of female John the Baptist, emerging as she did from the rural "wilderness" that separated the towns of Holland and Zeeland and preaching a coming judgment. Up and down Main Street her powerful voice reverberated from storefronts, carrying a clear message on how to escape God's wrath.

"Salvation is all of God's grace. You don't earn it by baptism, catechism, or church membership! You don't inherit it from your parents. Confess your sin and be born again by Jesus Christ into the family of God!" She quoted Bible proof texts such as "For by grace are ye saved through faith; and that not of yourselves, it is the gift of God—not of works, lest any man should boast" (Ephesians 2:8–9).

Ignoring the taunts of youngsters, Nellie stood tall in her black full-skirted, ankle-length dress with its high lace collar, shaking her long index finger at the Zeelanders and hoping the Truth would sink deeply into the hearts of some of her listeners.

Martin DeHaan was often among those who flocked after the street evangelist, but it was when he was about twelve years old that he felt as if the long, thin finger of Nellie Churchford had singled him out as the worst sinner in town. That day he didn't jeer with the rest of the kids, nor let on to anyone that the message had spoken to him. But as the buckboard creaked back toward Holland, with Nellie's husband at the reins, Martin trudged homeward with serious thoughts bombarding his boyish mind and heart. And sometime that afternoon, young Martin talked to God as he never had before. By faith, he wanted to be saved and be the kind of Christian Nellie Churchford talked about. He apparently didn't discuss this decision in detail with anyone, not even his parents or his pastor. This, he felt, was personal—between him and God.

It's not clear whether Martin had a genuine spiritual experience at this time; his life exhibited no marked change, although in later life he made occasional reference to this convicting moment. Nor is it known whether becoming a minister entered his mind at that time. Often when a young person comes face to face with the Eternal, he does have such thoughts. And if Martin had shared this news, his friends and his godly parents would have been pleased, for he was surrounded by hardworking, God-fearing people who delighted to see their sons and daughters become part of the church.

❋   ❋   ❋

The Dutch immigrants who settled in western Michigan, founding the towns of Holland and Zeeland, had a heritage deeply rooted in the Christian faith. The founders of Zeeland, like the seventeenth-century Pilgrim separatists, had traded persecution in their Netherlands homeland for a fresh start and a life of hardship in America in order that they might worship and serve God according to their beliefs. They were rugged individualists from Zeeland, the most southerly maritime province of the Netherlands, who for centuries had fought the sea and whose motto was "*Luctor et emergo*" ("I struggled and I emerge").

Trouble for them had begun in the Netherlands after the Crown established the state church in 1816. Influenced by the radical liberal theology of contemporary German thought, the church had developed a spirit of reckless free thinking and a dead formalism. Finally, in 1834, the loud protest of many pastors and their congregations resulted in secession and the establishment of the "Christelijk Afgescheiden Kerk" (Christian Seceded Church, later renamed Christian Reformed Church).

Persecution followed, though a royal decree in 1836 eased matters somewhat. The abused separatists began talking of emigration, and in September 1846 Albertus Christiaan Van Raalte, an enthusiastic young minister of the secession, sailed from Rotterdam for the United States with his family and forty-seven followers. In February 1847 they settled in western Michigan, founding the city of Holland. Next a body of prospective colonists in Zeeland completed a church organization, called Cornelius Van Der Meulen to be their pastor-leader, and 457 of them sailed for the States in the spring of 1847. Such a move by an emigrating group—coming as a complete church—had not been known since the days of the Pilgrims.

On June 27, after many had died from hardship and disease, the homesick Zeelanders arrived on a flat boat at Van Raalte's Holland. Jannes Van De Luyster, who had been a wealthy land owner in the province of Zeeland, then set up headquarters six miles east of the Holland settlement and proceeded to buy land at $1.25 an acre for a village to be called Zeeland. In his journal, Van De Luyster recorded the reason for the name: "Because it was founded by the Zeelanders, who called upon the name of the Lord to prosper His work, and that His name might be called upon there forever."

The Zeelanders worshiped for the first time there on the third Sunday in August 1847 under Dominie Van Der Meulen. Coached by those who had already conquered the wilderness, these Dutch settlers, with patience, perseverance, industry, and common sense, slashed out a rectangular village whose lots sold for $6.48 each. Here, for years to come, they would live under the able leadership of Jannes Van De Luyster, "the proprietor of the village of Zeeland," and Cornelius Van Der Meulen, the sympathetic, resourceful "Apostle of Zeeland."

Over the years, stories of the advantages of living in the Dutch colony in Michigan enticed more immigrants from the Netherlands, including twenty-two-year-old Reitze DeHaan, who came to Zeeland in the fall of 1881. The same year, fifteen-year-old Johanna Rozema, with several sisters and brothers, settled there.

In time Reitze became the town cobbler, but in those early years his thoughts were focused more on winning the hand of lovely Johanna than on mending shoes. A young man with an oval chin, a rather wide mouth, long sideburns, and oversized ears, he admired Johanna's industriousness and little stubborn

Dutch ways. There was nothing giddy about her and she loved the church as he did. Besides, there was much attractive about her: rather large blue eyes, a determined mouth, skin as delicate as a rose petal, and dark hair pulled tight and worn in a little knot; her figure pleased him, though she was ever so slightly taller than he was.

Reitze left his pedal stitcher and the smell of leather as he closed shop one day, and, with excitement surging within, hurried to ask Johanna the magic question. They were married in 1885, when she was nineteen and he, twenty-six. John was born a year later, followed in 1889 by a second son, Ralph.

Although Johanna longed for a girl, their third child, born on March 23, 1891, was another boy. She and Reitze decided he would be named after Reitze's brother, Martin, who worked with him at the cobbler's shop, and their third son was given the full name, Martin Ralph.

"Marty" was not quite ten when a daughter, Anna, was born to the DeHaans, but she died in infancy. Then a short time later a daughter was added to the family through adoption. It was the day before Christmas 1901 that Wiebe Vander Velde lost his wife in childbirth and found that five children were too much for him to care for by himself. The baby, Peter, went to relatives, while three-year-old Ada came to live with the DeHaans and was later legally adopted.

Ada was too young to remember her oldest adoptive brother, John, or his tragic drowning death, but years later she recalled the day-and-night difference between her brothers Ralph and Marty. "Ralph didn't care about worms and bugs and things like that, as Marty did. Their natures were different and they didn't even look alike. Ralph was thinner-faced and a little taller. In temperament he took more after my dad while Mart took after Mother, who was higher strung than Dad."

Marty, his sister said, once embarrassed his mother because of his keen interest in the insect world. As a boy of seven or eight, he was visiting with his mother in a home that was, as with many of the Dutch women, "crazy clean." Johanna DeHaan herself kept her home spotless, regularly brush-scrubbing woodwork and floor, and doing a thorough spring and fall housecleaning. But this woman went even further, washing the clothesline poles every week and keeping her house almost antiseptically clean. Thus both women were horrified when they discovered that Marty had brought flies in his pocket and was releasing them one by one, until the house was buzzing with the pests.

❋   ❋   ❋

In a real sense the Holy Scriptures were the center of the DeHaan home. With pious regularity Reitze read from the family Bible before each meal, followed by a substantial prayer, thanking God for supplying their needs and invoking His divine blessing. There was also a prayer of thanksgiving *after* every meal.

Around the table it was sometimes a babel, with three languages being spoken. When Reitze talked with Johanna, they usually spoke Frisian, their native dialect, a Low German tongue closely related to Anglo-Saxon. To the children the parents spoke Dutch, and the youngsters responded in English, which the parents understood but spoke with difficulty.

Like most other Zeelanders, the DeHaans were strict in their observance of Sunday. Reitze and Johanna regarded that day as the Sabbath, holy unto God, and all weekday activities ceased. The children dared not even play in the yard. On Sunday mornings the children were likely to awaken to the lusty voice of their father singing hymns and Dutch psalms as, with two fingers, he played the wheezy old reed organ downstairs. The family faithfully attended church three times on Sundays—morning, afternoon, and evening—where the relatively long services were in the Dutch language. The children went to catechism classes on Tuesdays, and these, too, were in Dutch.

During the first sixteen years of their married life, Reitze and Johanna were members of the First Christian Reformed Church in Zeeland. But following their eldest son's tragic death, the minister of their church didn't come to see them to offer comfort and help, whereas the pastor of the First Reformed Church showed special kindness to the family. The DeHaans soon placed their membership in the First Reformed Church, which dated back to the founding of Zeeland, its first pastor having been Dominie Van Der Meulen.

From time to time young Marty would visit his father's cobbler shop and chat with him and his Uncle Martin, who was a man with fascinating ideas. Uncle Martin talked of his religious beliefs, ideas that weren't generally heard or appreciated around the local Dutch community. He was considered a bit of a heretic and took pleasure in it. Christ, he said, was going to return someday in bodily form, just as He had been received into heaven following His resurrection; He could come any day. When that happened, believers were to be taken up to be with Jesus—the dead were to be raised, and the living were to follow them to be forever with Him. After a seven-year tribulation period on earth, Christ, with many of His followers, would set up a thousand-year kingdom on earth, over which He would rule from Jerusalem, asserted Uncle Martin, who shared with his nephew proof of his beliefs from a well-worn Bible.

While all this intrigued Marty, he didn't become a follower of Uncle Martin and his ideas. Instead, he loved exploring and learning what life was all about. He continued to collect insects and look for frogs along the edge of the cedar swamp in back of his house. He enjoyed studying the habits of animals and watching birds in flight.

He also enjoyed talking with his friends, though he was generally regarded as something of a loner. He and his buddies would gather at the railroad tracks, where they sat and discussed everything from the facts of life to theology. One boy from the gang ran away to the nearby city of Grand Rapids and returned with the story that he had heard a minister who seemed to doubt that the Bible was truly God's inspired Word—at least not all of it.

"We began to bat that around, and it was one of the most helpful discussions in this teenage period of my life," recalled D. J. (Dirk) De Pree, a boyhood friend of Martin DeHaan. "This conversation made us wonder if everything preached in our town was right. I don't definitely remember Martin in these conversations, but I imagine he was there. We had a gang and he was in it."

Martin was "one of the best students in the class," De Pree said. "In our day, students usually took four years of Latin and two years of German. Martin did a minimum of homework and preparation, but our teacher, Miss Wilhelm, herself a German, was really impressed by the way he could stand up in class and give a free translation of German. Actually, he knew the Frisian language so well that when it came to German he had little problem, because of its similarity. This particularly appealed to the teacher."

Apparently Martin's keen mind was not as challenged as it might have been in school. Since occasionally he wasn't prepared with his lessons, he devised a standard trick to avoid looking bad during oral quizzes. Questions were written and displayed, and the teacher went from student to student to obtain the answers. Martin quickly calculated which question would be his, and if he didn't know the answer, he held his handkerchief to his nose and asked to be excused. "I have a nose bleed," he said. Those who knew him well snickered at his pretense.

During his high school years, Martin concluded that he should drop out of school and go to work. For at least a semester he worked for an aunt and uncle, but getting up at 4:30 a.m. to begin chores appealed to him less than the boredom of classes. So, heeding his parents' urgings, he returned to school.

By the time he was a teenager, Martin was a husky young man, stocky, thick-necked, with muscular legs and arms and shoulders that let you know he was a football player. His high school football team was coached by a young man from Hope College in nearby Holland, a brainy fellow named Paul De Kruif, who would later write such books as *Microbe Hunters* and *Hunger Fighters*.

Martin was a 180-pound combination of power and speed. But according to De Pree, who was also on the team, "We couldn't get Martin to keep in training as he should and play regularly." The climax of his last year, 1908, in high school athletics was a post-season game with one of the two city high schools of Grand Rapids. The city team's star player that day was, a year later, named center on the Michigan All-State High School team, but that day the big-city team was held scoreless while Martin continually plowed through their line, scoring the only two touchdowns of the afternoon. It was said that he almost single-handedly won the game for the Zeeland High School against a formidable team.

❈   ❈   ❈

During his high school years Martin showed little indication of what he might do as his life work. If Johanna and Reitze DeHaan hoped their youngest son would become a minister, as they had dreamed for their eldest son, they had little on which to base those hopes other than faith that God would someday call him. However, three men in the community, besides Uncle Martin, undoubtedly sowed seeds in his mind and heart that would later influence him.

One of these men was a veterinarian with whom Martin enjoyed riding and talking as the vet made calls on his animal patients. Another was Dr. Huizenga, a Zeeland physician, and the third was Huizenga's son George, a talented fellow who began writing stories for *The American Boy* magazine when he was still in school. A would-be minister who in 1911 dropped out of seminary because of an eye affliction, George was another Zeelander who had become sort of a heretic by Reformed standards. In seminary George had been assigned to write a paper against premillennialism, but his research convinced him that indeed the return of Christ would be premillennial. This affected his own life to the extent that he became a fervent Christian, doing personal witnessing on the streets of Zeeland and sharing Christ over fences with his neighbors. George told Martin things that he never forgot, things that later became especially meaningful to him, adding to what he had learned from Uncle Martin.

❊　　❊　　❊

One day a slick character came to town and set up in a hotel, hoping to make a few bucks off curious farmers and gawking schoolboys. The sign he displayed provoked interest: "How smart are you? What is your main talent? What does the future hold for you?" According to the sign, the world-renowned Doctor X. Y. Smartz (or some such name) could "tell all" by a simple reading of one's head.

Martin DeHaan and Dirk De Pree gazed with awe at the sign and couldn't resist the temptation. Soon, with great ceremony, the phrenologist was deftly feeling the conformation of the skull of one lad and then the other. To Martin he pronounced, "Someday, my boy, you will be a great public speaker! I predict great things for you. You will be eloquent, and many people will listen to you."

Later, the boys decided they would put the phrenologist to the supreme test. Returning to their homes, they changed into entirely different clothing, then again visited the skull reader.

Would his predictions be the same? To Martin's amazement, the man uttered the same pronouncement. He was to be a public speaker.

But Martin shrugged it off as a lot of foolishness. "Me? I'm going to be a doctor," he told Dirk De Pree.

CHAPTER 2

TEXTBOOKS AND A
BLUE-EYED DUTCH GIRL

"Behold, thou art fair, my love; behold, thou art fair."
SONG OF SOLOMON 4:1

It was 1909, the year that President William Howard Taft called a special session of Congress for passage of the Payne Bill, reducing high tariffs; the year that Bill Borden, Chicago heir to millions, graduated from Yale intending to go to China as a missionary to the Muslims; and the year that Martin DeHaan, the boy with "oratory bumps" on his head, finished Zeeland High School and contemplated his next step in life. His high brush-cut hair, manly, serious physiognomy, and sturdy, handsome physique made him look several birthdays older than his eighteen years. His blue eyes and well-shaped, determined mouth, inherited from his mother, seemed to indicate a desire to succeed in life. Whereas the itinerant phrenologist had predicted Martin would use his mouth to cast spells upon the masses, Martin, as he had told his friend Dirk De Pree, intended to practice medicine and talk on a one-to-one basis, doctor to patient.

While this news probably surprised and pleased Martin's parents, they had to borrow to send him to college, just as they had planned to do for their eldest son, John.

After a year at Hope College in nearby Holland, Martin in October 1910 boarded the steamer that plied Lake Michigan between Holland and Chicago. In his pocket was an acceptance letter from the College of Medicine of the University of Illinois.

This was Martin's first visit to Chicago, and, at that time, his farthest journey from home. In those days a Zeelander considered a twenty-five-mile trip to Grand Rapids, or even a seven-mile trip to Holland, something to talk about; so crossing Lake Michigan to Chicago seemed comparable to a voyage to the other side of the world. And Chicago must have awed Martin, with its tall buildings, clattering elevated trains, bustling activity, swarming, seething humanity of all races and colors, and, most terrifying to a small-town teenager, its reputation for evil. In some areas of the sprawling lusty metropolis, evil men lurked in the shadows, waiting to step out and mug a passerby for the change he carried in his pockets. Booze flowed freely, available in taverns and beer gardens on nearly every block. Tawdry women walked certain streets beckoning and smiling foolishly to men with fat wallets. Shootings were numerous and ruthless hoodlums fought the police and each other as they sought to prove that crime would bring rich rewards.

Chicago was a symphony of fall colors, and there was the smell of burning leaves on the near West Side as Martin began his medical studies. In those years the College of Medicine of the University of Illinois was housed principally in an imposing five-story, two-hundred-foot long brick and stone building at the corner of West Harrison and Honore Streets, opposite Cook County Hospital. Among the features were three lecture rooms with a seating capacity of two hundred each, a clinical amphitheater seating three hundred, and an assembly hall for up to seven hundred. It also contained laboratories for physiology, chemistry, materia medica, therapeutics, and microscopical and chemical diagnosis, each capable of accommodating from fifty to one hundred students. A three-story annex building contained other laboratories and, according to a catalog of that day, "a supply of microscopes, lenses, oil immersions, and a projection apparatus for the illustration of lectures by means of stereopticon views."

The tough program of instruction at this school was "designed to teach the scientific method, to promote learning by problem-solving, and to develop the skills and attitudes of a mature physician." For a young man with only one year of college, it meant hard study.

Fortunately Martin DeHaan had a photographic mind, able to read a page quickly and recall its contents in detail. His medical books, if stacked on top of each other, likely would have reached the high ceiling of the school library, and he often studied into the early hours of the morning, memorizing endless lists of details relating to anatomy, biochemistry, physiology, histology, pathology, pharmacology, and many other subjects. Since University of Illinois medical students in those days did not go through internship, they did a great deal of clinical work, getting practical experience along with classroom instruction.

By no means did Martin neglect his church life during his medical school years. His mother, worried about her son in wicked Chicago, wrote Dr. John Van Peursem, pastor of a Reformed church in the area, and he took Martin under his wing, encouraging, challenging, and advising him. Martin joined the church and sang in the choir, lending his strong bass to cantatas in which choir members wore Dutch costumes.

＊   ＊   ＊

During his four years in Chicago, Martin carried out one especially enjoyable activity after he closed his medical books for the night: writing a thrice-weekly letter to Priscilla Venhuizen.

Martin had met Priscilla at a wedding in Holland during his year at Hope College when he was nineteen and she, sixteen. Priscilla, a pretty blue-eyed brunette who wore her hair in an upsweep, was full of life, and Martin had escorted her home following the wedding festivities.

"Things progressed nicely after that," Priscilla later recalled. When Martin was home in Zeeland, he pedaled a bicycle or rode the interurban train, sort of a Toonerville trolley, to call on her. Their dates consisted mainly of buggy rides.

In many respects, Martin's and Priscilla's backgrounds were similar, resting solidly on Reformed theology and tradition. A devout, ramrod-straight man with a mustache and goatee, Priscilla's father, William Venhuizen, went to church whenever the doors opened and made the Bible the center of their home.

During his first semester at school in Chicago, Martin was already saving money to buy an engagement ring for Priscilla. To help do so he skipped breakfast and skimped on lunch, subsisting on soup to which he added water and an extra amount of crackers. His no-breakfast plan became a habit that lasted for years, but once he had purchased the ring he began eating normal lunches.

Home for Christmas that year, Martin shoved medicine far from his thoughts and headed for Priscilla's. She had invited him for dinner, but he couldn't wait and arrived early to present her with the ring he had sacrificed to buy—a modest diamond in a yellow-gold tiffany setting. They then began to lay plans for their wedding on June 25, 1914, following his graduation from medical school.

※ ※ ※

Martin worked hard at his studies during the next four years, preparing for the day he would go into medical practice. On May 21, 1914, he traveled to Lansing, the state capital of Michigan, to appear before the state medical board. Though he faced this august body with some apprehension, he did well, receiving an average of 90.4% on the following subjects: anatomy, physiology, chemistry, pathology, materia medica, therapeutics, toxicology, histology, practice of medicine, surgery, obstetrics, mental and nervous diseases, diseases of the eye, ear, nose, and throat, bacteriology, hygiene, and public health laws of Michigan.

Priscilla made the trip by steamer across Lake Michigan to attend Martin's graduation. There was probably no prouder person in the Studebaker Theater that morning of June 11 for the 32nd Annual Commencement of the University of Illinois College of Medicine than Priscilla Venhuizen, because following the conferring of degrees by Dr. Edmund Janes James, president of the university, the valedictory was delivered by Martin Ralph DeHaan, M.D. At twenty-three, he was the youngest of his class of 111.

Two weeks later, on Thursday, June 25, Martin and Priscilla's wedding day dawned bright and warm. Priscilla excitedly directed the last-minute details for the wedding, which was to be held in the front yard of her family home on the outskirts of Holland. Members of the family helped by picking daisies from along the railroad tracks, and shortly before the ceremony erected a lattice of ferns and daisies beneath a large maple tree.

Then at 6:00 p.m. young Doctor DeHaan and Priscilla Venhuizen, dressed in her white gown with a long train, stood before Dr. John Van Peursem, Martin's Chicago pastor who now pastored a church in the area. Two little flower girls stood by, and William Venhuizen gave his daughter away. A soft breeze rustled the leaves on the maple tree, and the Venhuizen cow grazed peacefully nearby as Dr. Van Peursem uttered the meaningful words: "And now, by the authority vested in me as a minister of the Gospel and the laws of the state of Michigan, I do solemnly pronounce you to be husband and wife."

Following the wedding dinner, Dr. and Mrs. Martin DeHaan rode the interurban to the lakeside town of Muskegon, thirty-four miles to the north, where they spent several days honeymooning at the home of Benjamin Oosterbaan, a cousin of Martin's. Among other enjoyable summertime activities, they did a bit of boating, and they also were pestered a bit by the Oosterbaans' eight-year-old son, Bennie, who would grow up to become one of the greatest football players in the storied history of University of Michigan football and would, among other achievements, coach the Wolverines from 1948–1958.

Following their honeymoon, the newlyweds returned to Holland to face reality.

"All we had was debt when we married. We were so poor we couldn't even afford to have pictures taken," Priscilla said, remembering those early days. "Martin had every intention of repaying his father for sending him through medical school, and ultimately he did so."

At this point Martin had no idea where he would practice, although he wanted to stay in the area. And above all he wanted to live up to his class motto: *"Prodesse Quam Conspiceri"* (to be of service rather than to be in the limelight).

CHAPTER 3

COUNTRY DOCTOR

"To every thing there is a season . . . a time to be born,
and a time to die . . . and a time to heal. . . ."
ECCLESIASTES 3:1–3

In late summer of 1914, newsboys on the street corners of big cities had plenty to shout about. In the world of sports Jim Thorpe was in his heyday, Babe Ruth made his debut with the Boston Red Sox as an ace pitcher, Jack Dempsey was emerging as the big name in boxing, and Barney Oldfield was a household name among auto racing fans. In more serious news, President Woodrow Wilson and his Secretary of State, William Jennings Bryan, began a parting of the ways as they discussed the role of the U.S. in relation to a general European war that had ignited from a squabble between Austria and Serbia, crowding Wilson's domestic issues off front pages of American newspapers. This, of course, was the beginning of World War I.

But in the little country town of Byron Center, Michigan, fourteen miles due east of Zeeland, the big news was that young Martin DeHaan, M.D., was coming to hang out his shingle. Townspeople and farmers in the surrounding area had become disillusioned with one doctor, and the town's other M.D. couldn't handle everyone.

Actually, a letter to Martin's parents from an unhappy patient in Byron Center brought "Doc," as he was becoming known to his friends and family, to the little farming community. In a borrowed horse and buggy, he and Priscilla drove out to investigate. He had already looked into one or two other practice opportunities in the general area, but when he visited Byron Center and talked with the people he was soon convinced that this was his town.

The day Doc arrived with a wagonload of equipment and furniture, a patient was waiting on the front porch of the big two-story faded-red house on Main Street that he had rented. Others began coming in the following days, even before he and Priscilla could put the house in order.

The parlor served as Doc's office, and the living room as the waiting room; when it overflowed, patients sat on the stairway to the second floor. Among other things, the office contained a sterilizer heated by an alcohol flame, an examining table, and a medicine box from which Doc dispensed his medicines. The house was heated by three potbellied stoves, and with no electricity, the DeHaans used old-fashioned kerosene lamps to light the office and other rooms.

Doc added to their debt when he borrowed to buy a horse and buggy, and a cutter to be used in winter. Later, he added a Model T Ford to his means of transportation, but it could be used only when the rutty, narrow roads were dry, which was mainly in summer and early fall.

In time he was able to pay his debts, including the money he owed his father for his schooling. Actually, the money came surprisingly rapidly, although in his first year or so charges for his medical work seem ridiculously low when compared to modern-day rates: 50¢ for an office call, 50¢ or 75¢ for a house call, and $7.50 for an obstetrics case.

Within the first year of his practice, young Doctor DeHaan, now wearing a mustache for a more mature look, was treating patients from a wide area of the flat farm country. In making house calls, he quickly learned every shortcut. Hour after hour, day after day, through rain, sleet, snow, and summer drought, he drove his Ford, buggy, or cutter to bring medical help and comfort to residents of the area.

A spring day might find him driving his creaking, mud-splattered black buggy six miles or more through a driving March rain to reach patients as far north of Byron Center as Grandville, Wyoming, and Southwest Grand Rapids; the next day the ringing of the long-necked wall phone might send him ten miles west to Vriesland, five miles east into the Cutlerville area, or eight miles south to Dorr. Rarely, however, did he go out for single calls. Usually he made several calls during one trip, and on certain days he saw patients at a designated place, usually a home graciously offered for the purpose. And more than once, in an emergency, someone rushed Doc to a patient by handcar on the interurban railroad tracks.

These were adventurous but body-wearying days, even for a young man, and Doc often, after being out late the night before on calls, wasn't ready for his early-morning patients. Usually these were people who came into town with milk for the local creamery, and their farm wagons would begin stopping in front of the DeHaan home before 7:00 a.m. Priscilla, always an early riser, greeted them and assured them that the doctor would be ready to see them shortly. Sometimes she had to stir him a second time before he rolled out of bed, splashed cold water on his face, and dressed.

Fortified with a cup of strong, black, steaming coffee, however, Doc was soon bursting with energy and drawing wisely on his medical knowledge and common sense to try to cure disease and alleviate pain. Though rather brusque in his manner, he handled patients gently, talking to them at length, listening to their problems, and doing all within his means to meet their needs. Those means were not vast, as they are today. When it came to basic medications, he had only three: aspirin, morphine, and digitalis.

For all practical purposes, the era of modern medicine was still in its early stages. And while great advances were being made, questionable medications were being used by doctors everywhere. Horse-and-buggy doctors, as well as big-city physicians, prescribed both good and questionable vegetable drugs: among them, asafetida, cajuput, cannabis indica, camomile, croton oil, creosote, clove, mustard, spearmint, squill, and valerian, all of which have long gone out of style for one reason or another. How many of these Dr. DeHaan dispensed to his patients, the records do not tell. But what he did use he believed in, and when he prescribed remedies for his patients, he fully expected them to follow directions. For example, he was a great believer in mustard plasters for respiratory ailments, and magnesium sulphate (Epsom salts) was his standard remedy for several ailments, helpful especially for relieving the system of excess fluids.

It was Epsom salts prescribed by Doc that presumably saved the life of his sister Ada.

"I had diphtheria and was very sick," she recalled. "I was twenty-one at the time and still living in Zeeland. Our doctor gave me a shot but it didn't help. I got worse, and the folks wanted Mart to see me. But we didn't have telephone service during the day, so they had to wait till after six o'clock to call him. He got there about nine o'clock and gave me Epsom salts and that did the trick. It relieved the water that was backing up in my kidneys. The medicine the Zeeland doctor had given me was good, but he hadn't given me enough, and it was too slow-acting."

Epsom salts also saved the day—and a lot of painful scratching—for Maynard Vander Zaag, a neighbor youth who drove regularly for Doc from late fall to spring for several years.

"One time the itch was going around, and I got it on my thigh and began scratching till it bled. Doc was making up a sulfur salve and putting it in jars for patients with this annoying itch. 'Here, put this on,' he'd say, 'and leave your underwear on till the itch is gone. But put the salve on every day.'

"Well," Vander Zaag said, chuckling as he told of the incident, "a guy's underwear would get stiff as a board, till it could stand on end, and I didn't want any of that. So I told Doc I wanted something else. 'Look, Doc, I can't sleep nights, but give me something else besides that sulfur salve,' I said. Well, he told me to go home and dissolve as much Epsom salts in hot water as I could and to sponge the affected area. 'That'll take care of it,' Doc promised.

"I followed his directions, and I bet I dissolved at least a pound of Epsom salts in hot water. I took my sponge bath, and then paced the floor for about fifteen minutes till the sting went away. The next morning my brother asked, 'How did you sleep last night?' 'Like a baby,' I said. Then I told him about the Epsom salts, and he decided to try it because he had the itch too. Well, he tried it and I heard him hollering as he did it (boy! did that stuff sting!). But it cured him. After that he slept too."

An episode of a more serious nature involving his youthful driver features Dr. DeHaan in the role of surgeon and reveals the conditions under which he sometimes had to operate. It all started the evening Maynard's mother called Doc over to see the youth, who was suffering severe abdominal pains.

"Minnerd," Doc said after examining him—it was never Maynard with Doc, always Minnerd— "it could be appendicitis. I don't know for sure, but we're going to keep an eye on this thing."

Doc called for the standard treatment of that period, prescribing that hot bags of salt be applied to the abdomen throughout the night. Then, after examining Maynard the next morning, he ordered a switch to ice packs, hoping to reduce the inflammation if it was appendicitis, or stop the muscle spasm if that was the problem. This seemed to remedy the ailment, as the pain subsided. However, a few days later Maynard complained of pain again, and Doc announced that an appendectomy was imperative.

But Maynard's mother balked. Operations were dangerous. And she didn't want her son going off to the hospital in Grand Rapids. If it had to be done, couldn't it be done at home? Doc said it could, though he preferred to do it in the hospital. Finally he agreed to operate in the home, with the assistance of a Grand Rapids surgeon. But still Maynard's mother hesitated.

Doc turned to the boy. "Minnerd, do you want an operation or not? We'll let you decide."

Maynard allowed that he'd "never be any good this way anyhow—may as well take 'er out, Doc."

"We'll be here tonight at eight o'clock," Doc told Maynard's mother.

"Bring me a pretty nurse," the perky patient joshed.

"You leave the nurse to me," Doc said, a twinkle in his eye, and disappeared out the door.

The nurse he brought that night wasn't exactly what Maynard had in mind, but "she was a fine nurse," said Vander Zaag. Doc also brought the surgeon, Dr. Lyman, with him, and they rigged up lights in the dining room with the aid of a battery from the garage. The nurse scrubbed the dining room table antiseptic clean, Maynard stretched out on the table, Doc administered ether, and the operation was underway.

After the appendix was out and the patient in bed, Doc gave orders that the boy needed rest for ten days. "I'll keep an eye on him," Doc said. "He's my driver and we've got to take good care of him and get him back on his feet."

❋   ❋   ❋

Interestingly, Dr. DeHaan lacked the long, thin hands generally associated with a surgeon. His hands were rather chubby with stubby fingers, but he used them expertly in his surgery, just as he did in later years as a fly fisherman. According to one of his fishing companions, "He was an expert at tying a fly onto the line. Just a few movements and he had it done quick as a wink."

Most of Doc's surgical work was done in the hospital in Grand Rapids, but some was performed in his office or in a patient's home. "It was the minor, traumatic type, such as a farm worker cutting off a finger, that he did in the home or in his office," his son Marvin, who himself became a physician, later recalled from conversations with his father. "When he was required to operate in a home, he used relatives and friends to help. He carried all the necessary instruments and other items with him—scalpel, hemostats, needles, sutures, gauze—prepared for an emergency. He used thread that had been boiled for suture material.

"Also, he generally did tonsillectomies in his office. I'm still amazed at how tonsils were taken out, and how they were able to do it without hemorrhaging," says Marvin. "I think he looped a wire around the tonsil; then a pull on the wire snipped it off. He then put a pack in to stop the bleeding. It must have taken a lot of nerve to do things that way."

Nothing brought the Doctor as much delight as ushering new lives into the world, but these adventures in obstetrics cost him many sleepless nights and other hardships. The night deliveries, at least in his earlier years of practice, were done by the light of kerosene lamps, and generally he worked without assistance, except a helping hand from a family member.

At times he battled howling storms to reach women in labor. The winter of 1914–15 was probably the worst. Some of the storms were so fierce that even the steam and electric railway traffic in nearby Grand Rapids was all but paralyzed. But icy winds, zero temperatures, and snow didn't stall the country doctor, for babies wouldn't wait. Dressed in his bearskin coat and fur cap, a horsehide blanket over his lap and a heated soapstone or lighted lantern at his feet, undaunted, Dr. DeHaan traveled the dangerous roads day and night in a cutter pulled by a faithful horse.

Once, on a frosty night, Maynard Vander Zaag drove the Doctor in the sputtering Model T to a farm home where a German woman was in labor. Usually in such situations Maynard remained outside, but after a few minutes Doc opened the door and called, "Minnerd, it's probably going to be a long wait. Better drain the water out of the radiator and bring some blankets in and get some rest on the kitchen floor."

"I tried to sleep but I couldn't," Vander Zaag recalled. "I heard this woman taking on, and her husband was in the kitchen with me, beside himself, pacing the floor. Then all at once we heard a baby cry, and his face brightened. With a German accent, he bellowed in relief, 'I'm glad that's over with!' Then pretty soon we heard another one cry, too. 'My goodness, that's seven kids in six years!' he moaned. Now he began pacing the floor not knowing what to do, for he was quite poor."

Vander Zaag added, "I've got to give Doc credit—if they were poor people, he'd do a case like that for almost nothing. He'd cut the $7.50 price way down. He was really good-hearted."

Sometimes people paid their medical bills in farm products. On one occasion, after Doc cared for a farmer who had broken his leg, he learned the man was going to sell his cow to pay the bill. But Doc told him to consider his account paid—the cow was the man's only source of milk and butter for his family.

✻　✻　✻

On June 1, 1916, young Dr. DeHaan delivered a very special baby—his first child, Ruth. As would be true with the births of all their children, another physician attended Priscilla during her pregnancy, but her husband performed the delivery.

In later years, Dr. DeHaan delighted in meeting the grown-up children that he had delivered, and he enjoyed telling about the twins "born a year apart," as he termed it. He was reminded of the incident forty-eight years later when he was shopping in a hardware store. A man came up to him, shook his hand, and said, "You are Dr. DeHaan, I believe. You attended my first 'birthday party.' In fact, you were the master of ceremonies." Then he went on to remind Doc that he had attended his mother when he and his twin brother were born—one at 11:50 p.m., December 31, 1916, and the other on January 1, 1917, at 12:15 a.m.

"Yes, indeed, I remember!" exclaimed Dr. DeHaan. "It was quite a noisy New Year's party, especially after I gave the two of you your first spankings."

But what thrilled Dr. DeHaan even more than being reminded of the incident was the news that the twin brothers each had had another birthday. On the same night eighteen years later, both had been born again of the Spirit of God in a gospel meeting.

"For my father, obstetrics was either a lot of fun or tragic," said Marvin DeHaan, recalling medical shoptalk with his father. "Birth can be an easy procedure. But if he were to get into a situation with a massive hemorrhage he had two lives at stake within a very few minutes. He would have parents who had been expecting this wonderful new life for nine months, and then suddenly there's a problem. I know he had some tragic situations where both the child and mother died."

Despite his rugged constitution, Doc sometimes felt drained of strength and much in need of rest following a protracted vigil at the bedside of an expectant mother, or after a long day of house calls. On occasion he got some sleep in a home, or, on calls, in the back seat of the Model T while Maynard drove. Often on routine calling days he didn't get home till nearly midnight, and there were times he returned home on Sunday morning in time to nod a greeting to neighbors on their way to church.

Once he was so weary he fell asleep while driving the cutter, and the outcome could have been tragic. "It was in the early hours of a February morning," Doc said, "when I was coming home in my cutter. The weather was bitter cold and my legs were wrapped in a heavy robe, with a lighted kerosene lantern between my feet. I pulled the collar of my bearskin coat around my head and fell fast asleep. Toots, a small bay mare who knew the way home, plodded on. Suddenly I awoke to hear the roar of a locomotive! I sat up—and, lo, Toots had heard the train coming and had stopped about twenty-five feet from the track."[1]

---

1. *Our Daily Bread*, March 19, 1963.

It was well known that Doc loved his horses, especially gentle, intelligent Toots. But he even had affection for Boob, "a big, black, one-eyed brute who was the dumbest creature I ever knew," said Maynard Vander Zaag. Undoubtedly his favorite, however, was Billy, the first horse he owned, and the friskiest.

Billy was the type of horse that couldn't be stopped, giving a second effort when the cutter hit a dry spot in the road, pulling it across with seemingly little effort. The more Doc drove Billy, the wilder Billy got. But Doc vowed he'd never sell him. "I'll keep Billy as long as he lives," he once told Maynard. One day, to Doc's sorrow, however, Billy made his last house call with his owner, dropping dead on the road. For years a painting of the majestic, chestnut Billy hung in Dr. DeHaan's study.

In many respects, the country doctor himself was a man with the nature of Billy—full of zest, forging ahead against obstacles that would stop most men, and, yes, even a bit frisky at times. People in the area were glad he had chosen to settle in Byron Center, and they were to be especially grateful for such a doctor during the terrifying days of the flu pandemic of 1918–19.

CHAPTER 4

THE PANDEMIC

"And there was a great cry in Egypt . . . ."
EXODUS 12:30

A biting west wind of up to twenty-five miles per hour, picking up moisture from Lake Michigan, dumped fifteen inches of snow on the Byron Center area in mid-January 1918, adding to seven inches already on the ground. Then the mercury dipped to fourteen degrees below zero. Country roads were blocked with snowdrifts for days, but twenty-six-year-old Dr. Martin Ralph DeHaan, deferred from duty in World War I because he was needed on the home front, made his house calls as usual, riding his cutter as far as he could go to reach a home, then blanketing down his horse and hiking the rest of the way on foot.

But the greatest challenge of his medical career was yet to come, and it wasn't to be weather. It started innocently enough in June of that year when he examined a patient who complained of a headache, fever, and prostration.

"You've got a case of old-fashioned flu," said Doc. "Aspirin, plenty of liquids, and rest. You should be all right in a few days."

Unknown then to Byron Center's busy doctor, thousands of other doctors in Michigan, across the United States, and around the world were encountering similar cases.

The first wave of the notorious influenza pandemic hit in June and July; cases were numerous but few died from the disease. Then came a second wave in October and November as millions around the world fell victim to a more potent form of influenza. After contracting the malady, about one-fifth of the patients died—within hours in many instances. Then, in February 1919, a third wave swept the world, and the disease this time was fatal—especially to youths and young adults. In the U.S. alone during the prolonged pandemic, an estimated 20 million persons contracted the disease and some 450,000 died. The influenza pandemic was also associated with the rise of mortality from other respiratory diseases such as whooping cough and tuberculosis.

"People fell like sticks before a tornado," Dr. DeHaan wrote later. "In some families eight, nine, or ten were sick at the same time. Some also had pneumonia. Outside, the temperature hovered around zero. From everywhere the calls for help came, and we were unable to reach many for several days. For five days and nights at a time I never took off my clothes, but snatched a bit of sleep in the car while being driven, or on a couch while waiting for a baby to be born of a mother with a fever of 105 degrees."[1]

Maynard Vander Zaag, Doc's driver, recalled that he put in the longest day of his life with the doctor during the second wave of the pandemic. They worked from 5:00 a.m. one day until 5:00 the next morning. They began the day by driving the Ford to North Dorr, south of Byron Center, to pick up a young woman with appendicitis. After taking her to a hospital

---

1. *Our Daily Bread*, September 14, 1959.

in Grand Rapids, Dr. DeHaan assisted another surgeon in the operation. Then Maynard drove Doc back to the Byron Center area, where Doc made some forty to fifty house calls to treat flu victims.

One of his remedies in treating flu cases was the mustard plaster—a paste mixture of powdered mustard, flour, and water sandwiched in a cloth—used when victims developed respiratory problems.

"He was one of the best flu doctors in the whole area," commented a contemporary. "He lost fewer patients than any doctor that I know of. He seemed to have the right idea with that mustard plaster. I know. When I'd get a cold that I couldn't break, I'd get a mustard plaster and that usually fixed me up."

There was one bright spot during those dark days of the flu epidemic. On March 25, 1919, the DeHaan's second child, June, was born. And once again, Doc was the attending obstetrician.

❄ ❄ ❄

There was nothing Doc DeHaan enjoyed more than his medical work. He was in his element while diagnosing and treating patients. When the crank of a Model T kicked back, breaking the owner's arm, the Doctor delighted in being of service. Once he was called to save the lives of an entire family when a mother inadvertently added lead arsenate to her pancake batter. He felt a purpose was being fulfilled in his life as he answered these emergency calls.

Probably one of the most rewarding diagnoses he ever made was for his own mother. While she was visiting him once in Byron Center, Martin looked at her and asked, "Were you crying? Your eyes are red." When she said no, he examined her carefully and concluded that diabetes had been the problem bothering her for years. Insulin had recently been discovered, and he put her on it, giving her a new lease on life.

As far as Martin R. DeHaan, M.D. knew, he would be a country doctor all his days. He and Priscilla had bought a home in 1919, better suited to a doctor's practice than the house on Main Street. Among other more modern facilities, it had battery-powered electricity and a furnace. But before long, a series of events began that would change the course of his life drastically.

In October 1921, Doc experienced an unusual toothache. At first it seemed to be a problem for a local dentist, but his condition worsened and he was hospitalized in Grand Rapids. The tooth was extracted, and he was given an injection containing horse serum. Within a day after he had returned home, his system reacted violently to the serum. Hives covered his body and his eyes swelled shut. Suffering much pain and discomfort, he was readmitted to the hospital in critical condition.

Although he recovered and returned home a few days later, he returned a different person—one with the same rugged exterior, but a man with new goals, the beginning of new attitudes, and a new life within. During his years as a physician, some of Martin's patients showed their hospitality by giving him wine, hard cider, and liquors when he made house calls. Over time the Doc had become known not only for his medical skill, but also for his drinking problem. Now, the Lord would begin to deal with him concerning this and other habits.

The wonderful transformation that had begun would, however, also bring sorrow to the people of the Byron Center area. For because of it, their beloved physician would terminate his practice and, under God's leading, begin a new career that would ultimately find him doctoring spiritual ills of people around the world.

CHAPTER 5

A New Man

"Therefore, if any man be in Christ, he is a new creature. . . ."
2 CORINTHIANS 5:17

A s thirty-year-old Martin Ralph DeHaan, M.D. struggled
for life in October 1921 in a Grand Rapids hospital, he did
considerable thinking about his past—and about his future.

For all of his life he had been identified with the church.
As a boy he had attended church regularly, and even in medical school he had been faithful in attendance. After their marriage, he and Priscilla had joined the Byron Center Reformed
Church, and he had attended when he could. But he realized
that his life hadn't been counting for God as it should have.
There were sins in his life at which God's finger was pointing,
and he felt condemned, even though as a twelve-year-old boy
he had presumably settled his relationship with God.

It was in that hospital room that a quiet transaction took
place in the heart and life of the young doctor-patient. In 1929
he penned these words: "I was born in 1891 of the flesh, 'a child
of wrath even as others.' After a life of sin for thirty-one years,
I was born again of the Spirit in October 1922. Since then my

only hope and aim is to exalt Him to whom be all glory forever and ever (Ephesians 1:7)."[1]

Priscilla, who learned of her husband's spiritual experience when she visited him in the hospital shortly after it happened, recalled that as he talked about it afterward he mentioned that he wasn't sure he had truly met God at age twelve. The hospital experience was a spiritual struggle not unlike the Old Testament patriarch Jacob's, who wrestled with God until dawn before he received a new touch and blessing from the divine hand. "Spare my life and I'll serve You," Martin pleaded with God. And evidently he meant it with all his heart, for after he went home a few days later and soon resumed his practice, he did so with a new awareness of God. Now there were quiet conversations about the future—and about how Martin would fulfill his pledge of service.

Neighbors soon noticed the difference. The DeHaans were among the few families who owned a phonograph, and, according to a longtime resident of Byron Center, "When their windows were open, we could hear such songs as 'Since Jesus Came into My Heart.'"

Farmers in their fields and children at play, and even his horses, must have wondered what had happened to Doc, for from time to time his wife accompanied him on house calls and they could be heard singing glad songs of the faith as they rode along like a honeymooning couple in the buggy. "He had such joy in his heart that he liked to sing about it," recalled Priscilla.

---

1. From all indications, Dr. DeHaan's memory played a trick on him. He was in seminary in the fall of 1922 and living in Holland, according to records of Western Theological Seminary and the American Medical Association. Thus he was thirty when his conversion occurred in October 1921.

It wasn't only knowledge of sins forgiven that made Doc burst with joy. This was enough, to be sure. But the idea that he was going to serve God brought great delight to him. He felt that, in a sense, he was stepping into the shoes of his brother John, who had drowned before seeing his—and his parents'—dream of becoming a minister fulfilled. When Martin told his mother the news, she wept with joy. God had answered her prayers concerning her youngest son's waywardness, and He was also, at last, giving her a minister-son. He was blessing her beyond measure.

Martin gave much credit to his mother for what had happened to him. "I was blessed with a godly, praying mother," he said in later years, "and her admonitions have never left me. I can still close my eyes and in memory see her kneeling at her bed, wiping the tears from her eyes with her blue-checkered apron. Oh, precious, blessed memories! It was Mother's prayers which influenced me more than all the preaching to which I was exposed with unfailing regularity."

He also wrote with a grateful heart of his father. "His life of prayer, his study of the Word, his faithful habit of teaching his children are memories more precious than I can tell."

As the weeks passed, Martin talked with Priscilla—and with God—about the kind of Christian service he should do. Preach? Become a missionary? He wasn't sure. He talked about going abroad as a missionary, but friends pointed out that he could continue his medical practice, be God's man on the job, and at the same time support a missionary. For a time he thought perhaps this was the answer.

The matter continued to burden him increasingly, until finally, one day in early spring of 1922, he came in from his house calls and said to Priscilla, "I can't go on any longer." In an act of finality, he slid his medical bag across the kitchen floor. "This is it!"

He soon sold his practice, his office equipment, and his home, and made plans to enter Western Theological Seminary, the Reformed Church seminary in nearby Holland.

✳   ✳   ✳

The transformation in his life continued to amaze Martin DeHaan. As he read and studied his Bible, he saw it all as a matter of God's grace. In later years he was to make a careful study of the grace of God and pen these words on the subject: "Like electricity, light and life, we know only what it [grace] does, rather than what it is. Why God should choose the meanest, basest, most unworthy individuals with absolutely nothing to commend them at all to God, except their miserable, lost condition, and then exalt them to become the sons of God, members of the divine family, and use them for His glory, is beyond all reason and human understanding. Yet that is grace."

That Martin saw himself as the object of God's grace is illustrated by an incident that he related years later.

> Some time ago on my way to Colorado, I stopped off to visit my son Marvin on Chicago's North Side. After parking my car, I took a shortcut to the apartment, through one of Chicago's North Side alleys, and there amid the dust and the refuse and the filth and rats, I encountered one of the most pathetic sights I have ever beheld.
>
> There, beside a leaking barrel filled with garbage, and black with flies, stood one of society's outcasts, a man about sixty-five years old. Only the rim of his tattered hat was left, his shoes were tied on with rope, his coat in shreds,

his trousers in tatters, his hands black with filth, his hair matted together, his beard even worse. I watched him as he pawed about in the garbage, pulled out a whisky bottle with a teaspoon of its poison left, and lifted it to his lips. He found another drop or two in another bottle, and then he fished out a crust of garbage-sodden bread and placed it in his mouth with his filthy hands. As I stood there, I . . . said to myself, "O God, O God! That's me! That's me, apart from Thy wonderful grace." . . . Under similar circumstances of birth, environment and opportunity, I would have been no different, and no better. What a humbling truth grace is!

In experiencing God's grace, Martin found himself not only a sinner redeemed from hell and on the way to heaven, but also a man in whom God was making a difference. He was as human as ever and still a Hollander through and through. His temperament hadn't changed, and he realized he was subject to temptations as before. But his new God-implanted life was changing his perspective. He now had a ready source of victory: the indwelling Holy Spirit; a mighty Savior and Friend, Jesus Christ; and an omnipotent heavenly Father. In a real sense 2 Corinthians 5:17 was being worked out in his experience: "Therefore, if any man be in Christ, he is a new creature; old things are passed away; behold, all things are become new."

Perhaps the most marked example of triumph in Doc's life came one day shortly before he gave up his practice, when a grateful patient proudly presented a gift to the faithful physician—a bottle of liquor. Doc took the bottle home, and all the way the Holy Spirit tugged at his conscience. "You know how strong drink has made a fool of you," He seemed to say. "You've determined to give it up now that you are Christ's. Rely on Me; I'll help you."

When he showed the bottle to his wife, fear gripped her heart. How Priscilla had prayed that he would quit the miserable habit! But praise to God replaced her fear as Martin resolutely shook his head and said, "I don't dare keep it; it simply would not honor the Lord." Ceremoniously, he poured the contents of the bottle down the drain, dramatically signifying a mighty victory over a fleshly habit he had come to hate, but which he by himself had been unable to break. God had done it for him. He was free!

This did not mean, of course, that he did not have battles with other, often more subtle, forms of sin. For example, like a thorn in the flesh, his temperament, marked by occasional outbursts of temper, impetuosity, and what some termed "Dutch stubbornness," continued to keep him keenly aware that he had a lot of room to grow.

Once at a picnic, so the story goes, Doc hit a grounder in a baseball game and the umpire called him out at first base. Certain that he was safe, he argued till the ump and his own teammates finally turned away and continued the game, ignoring Doc on first. An inning or two later, when the call came for supper, the still-simmering DeHaan remained determinedly camped on first.

In 1954, in his book *Simon Peter*, Dr. DeHaan, pointing out that Peter was both a sinner and a saint, showed that the apostle Paul recognized a constant struggle between the evil nature and the new nature, citing Paul's statement in Romans 7:20: "Now if I do that I would not, it is no more I that do it, but sin that dwelleth in me."

"Paul wrote this thirty years after he had been saved and had become a new creation in Christ. He still realized his danger, he knew his need of help outside of himself, and he made no claim or boast of having gotten rid of the old man, once and for all.

Paul realized the hopelessness of battling in his own strength, and turned it all over to the Lord Jesus Christ for victory."

Dr. DeHaan continued by asserting that, whereas Paul claimed the victory, it did not imply that the flesh had been done away with or eradicated. Actually, he said, "the older it becomes, the more rotten it seems to be."

In his book *Law or Grace*, Dr. DeHaan berated those who consider themselves completely free from the power of sin. "Unfortunately, there are some poor, blind, mistaken people who claim sinless perfection. They tell us the old sinful nature has been eradicated, root and branch, and they never sin any more. To them the Lord Jesus Christ is wasting His time at the right hand of God as our interceding High Priest, for they have nothing to confess, and need no one to intercede for them." And he often made reference to his gratefulness to God for including 1 John 2:1 in the Bible: "If any man sin, we have an advocate with the Father, Jesus Christ the righteous."

Martin DeHaan, like Peter and Paul, laid his own frailties before the Lord as he doggedly served and worshiped Him.

Soon, however, even his stubbornness and staunch determination were to be harnessed as he stood strong against the leaders of his own denomination when he believed they were not following the clear teachings of the Bible. As a result, he would be branded a heretic by some and a heroic defender of the faith by others.

CHAPTER 6

TEMPEST IN GRAND RAPIDS

*"Preach the word; be instant in season, out of season; reprove, rebuke,
exhort with all long-suffering and doctrine."*
2 TIMOTHY 4:2

In the months after Martin decided to sell his practice in
Byron Center and enter seminary, he and Priscilla wrestled
with occasional doubts. Were they really doing the right thing?
If God wanted him in seminary, then why didn't He find suitable housing for them in Holland, where the seminary was sit-
uated? By late spring of 1922 they had spent many hours poring
over the classified ads in the local newspaper and knocking at
doors, but each trip to Holland brought only disappointment.

Finally, they were able to rent a furnished house from other
seminary students who were to be away for the summer, which
provided time for them to locate another available house to
rent for the duration of Martin's seminary years. Among the
items that Martin brought from Byron Center were his medical
bag and his reputation as a capable physician and surgeon. This
proved providential, for some of his former patients drove or
rode the interurban to Holland to see him, and others nearby
also knocked at his door for medical assistance.

A fellow seminary student, the Rev. Edward H. Tanis, recalled: "Following a bout that I had with tonsillitis, Doc recommended removal of my tonsils, and, along with another city physician, took them out right there in his office. DeHaan was a good doctor. Once he was a bit tardy for a class, and as he entered the classroom he held up two fingers. He had just delivered twins."

The DeHaans welcomed the income from this out-of-the-bag practice, aware that even with their substantial savings, Doc's three years in seminary would not be an easy matter financially, especially with their growing family. By this time, their daughter Ruth was a sprouting six-year-old, and June was three. Then, on February 21, 1923, as Martin settled into his studies at Western Theological Seminary, he delivered their third child, a baby boy, Richard William.

Likely on his first day back in seminary following his son's arrival, the proud young father wasn't fully tuned in on the lectures of such distinguished faculty members as Albertus Pieters, John R. Mulder, E. J. Blekkink, and John E. Kuizenga, the latter of whom spent the last seventeen years of his career at Princeton, where he was chairman of the Department of Theology. But Martin, with the keen mind that had won him valedictory honors in medical school, was a good student, retaining what he heard and understanding the material without difficulty.

During the summers of his seminary years, Martin pastored small churches. In 1923 he had a charge north of Holland, and in 1924 he served in Lafayette, Indiana. The first year he hammered hard at Modernism from the pulpit, an issue of growing concern in the 1920s, and the following summer he preached almost exclusively from the Heidelberg Catechism.

When he graduated in the spring of 1925, his family watched proudly, including his mother and father, who thanked God that they at last had a full-fledged pastor-son. (The godly Johanna lived only a year after Martin became a minister, dying on September 6, 1926, at the age of sixty, a victim of diabetes. Reitze, who had made a clear profession of faith in 1921, lived on to the age of seventy-two, dying after a brief illness on November 8, 1931.)

※   ※   ※

After his graduation from seminary, Dr. M. R. DeHaan received a call from Calvary Reformed Church in Grand Rapids. His ordination by the Reformed Church Classis of Grand Rapids was confirmed on May 21, 1925, "with great satisfaction to the Classis," and he was soon installed and assumed the pastorate of the established and flourishing Calvary Reformed Church on East Fulton Street in Grand Rapids.

The thirty-four-year-old DeHaan quickly began to attract large audiences. He was a good preacher, committed not only to teaching the Bible but also to calling lost sheep into the fold. His able preaching was enhanced by his booming, gravelly voice, unaided by electronic equipment.

Among those God drew to himself through Martin's strong evangelistic preaching was his own sister, Ada. She considered herself a Christian because she had learned the catechism and was a church member. But when she joined the crowds who flocked to hear her brother, she became increasingly uneasy; it seemed that his eyes were on her, almost searching out her soul. Yet in one visit he greeted her following a service, saying, "Why, Ada, I didn't know you were here."

At home on Sunday afternoons she listened to Martin preach on the radio to a citywide audience. The more she heard him, the more she doubted her salvation. He made it so clear that being a church member did not necessarily mean that an individual belonged to God's family. She vowed not to listen, but on Sundays her hand fell on the radio dial, and on came the deep, persuasive voice of her brother. Finally one Sunday afternoon, in March 1927, she said yes to Jesus Christ there beside her radio, depending wholly on Him for the eternal salvation of her spirit and not on works that she had done or on church membership.

Maynard Vander Zaag was another convert. "Minnerd, if anything happens to you, I'll figure it's my fault," Doc told his former driver one day, putting his arm around him. "I set you a pretty poor example."

Vander Zaag shook his head "no," for he had looked up to the Doctor in those days when he drove him to his house calls. Now, however, he was seeing a new Doc in action. And subsequently, in a service at Calvary Reformed, he placed his faith solely in the Savior. "I was one of those stiff church people up to that point," he said. "Doc helped me see what Jesus Christ was all about."

Exciting things were happening in Grand Rapids, to be sure, and one of those exciting events was the birth of Martin and Priscilla's fourth child, Marvin, on November 18, 1926.

❋   ❋   ❋

When M. R. DeHaan began pastoring at Calvary Reformed Church in 1925, the congregation numbered 182 members. By the spring of 1927 the congregation had grown to 360 members, and by the spring of 1928 an additional 223 new members had been added. Within two years, the church budget increased from $9,000 to more than $25,000, and twice between the years of 1925 and 1929 the church had to be remodeled because of the needs of the growing congregation. Frequently the church was packed to the doors with people standing along the aisles and in the stairwells to the balcony and to the basement.[1]

People came early to get seats, but not because of any gimmicks. The only extra attraction besides impassioned Bible teaching was a half-hour of congregational singing that warmed up early arrivals awaiting the regular service.

On Monday evenings, in addition to the midweek meeting, Dr. DeHaan taught Bible classes—from 7:00 to 8:00 for teenagers, and from 8:00 to 9:00 for adults. He took both groups deep into the Word of God, making once-dry portions come alive. Teens and adults alike looked upon him as the voice of authority, and youths loved him despite his strict ways.

Often on Friday evenings Dr. DeHaan himself attended a Bible class, termed the "largest weekday class in the world," at the Mel Trotter Mission in downtown Grand Rapids. Here he added to his knowledge of the Word as he heard Dr. Billy McCarrell, pastor of Cicero Bible Church near Chicago. Regularly some 2,000 people, including the mayor of Grand Rapids, filled the former theater building, with its three balconies, to hear the fundamental and hidden truths of the Bible expounded by the colorful, veteran teacher. DeHaan and McCarrell became warm friends through their common interest in the Bible.

As the voice and preaching style of M. R. DeHaan became even better known in the Grand Rapids area, another service was added on Sunday evenings at Calvary Reformed—an after-

---

1. Thomas Boslooper, *Grace and Glory Days* (Charlevoix/Clearwater: Woodswalker Books, 1990), 4.

service for those from other churches. "Many made decisions for Christ," Doc's old friend from his boyhood days, D. J. (Dirk) De Pree, recalled. "There was a deep moving of the Holy Spirit. This continued for several years. These were the days when the Doctor became a powerful preacher and teacher of the Word, and a widely known personality."

Dr. DeHaan moved about the platform freely, crashing his fist onto the pulpit frequently to punctuate a thought, his deep voice and exciting messages riveting listeners to their seats. He once became literally lost in communion with God during the "long prayer" just prior to the sermon. When he finished he opened his eyes and found himself looking at the organ pipes behind the pulpit, his back to the audience. "This was so embarrassing that from then on when I prayed I always held on to the pulpit," DeHaan later said to a friend.

He increasingly sought to explore the depths of the Word of God, not being content merely to preach what he had learned in seminary. One of his most important "tutors" was the Scofield Reference Bible, with its extensive notes by C. I. Scofield and its dispensational, premillennial interpretation of the Bible. During this period, Dr. DeHaan also feasted on the Bible teaching of such men as William L. Pettingill, H. A. Ironside, James M. Gray, and William R. Newell.

It was the late Dr. Pettingill, one of the editors of the Scofield Reference Bible, to whom Dr. DeHaan gave credit for straightening him out on the relationship of law and grace. Pettingill, preaching at the invitation of DeHaan, declared that salvation had nothing to do with observance of the law. The law, he said, speaks of condemnation and judgment but has nothing to do with changing the heart. It's the grace of God that gives life. Grace plus nothing equals salvation, the visiting preacher emphasized.

Afterward, DeHaan, who had been reared on a strong dose of the Ten Commandments, approached him. "One of us is wrong, and if it's me I want to know it," he said. Pettingill shared with him the booklet *Rightly Dividing the Word of Truth* by C. I. Scofield, and this marked the beginning of what M. R. DeHaan deemed his clearer understanding of the doctrines of law and grace.

He stepped up his evangelistic appeal, and about the same time began to stir his congregation concerning the imminent return of Christ for His church. "This same Jesus, who came 1,900 years ago, may return at any moment," he declared. "His second coming is mentioned 240 times in the New Testament alone, more times by far than any other doctrine in the entire Bible. The exact day of this great event, however, has not been revealed."

Many listeners dared not leave the services before making sure of their relationship to God. Some wept and agonized before they had assurance that they were saved and would be among those caught up to be with the Lord. They wanted to be with Christ, reigning, when He set up His millennial kingdom upon the earth, for Dr. DeHaan thundered that, according to the clear teachings of Scripture, the coming again of the Lord Jesus Christ would not be the end of the world.

"The end of the *age* and the end of the *world* are two entirely different events, separated by a great period of time," he explained. "The end of the world will not occur until at least 1,000 years after the end of this present age. The end of the *age* will come when our Lord returns for His Church. After a brief period of tribulation, He will cleanse the earth and judge His enemies. Then, our Lord will set up His messianic, millennial kingdom upon the earth, and the saints will reign with Him."

A number of Christians in western Michigan had already been introduced to this premillennial view, but to many others, particularly from the Reformed tradition, Dr. DeHaan preached of "things to come" that were excitingly new.

❈   ❈   ❈

Despite the growth, both numerically and spiritually, at Calvary Reformed Church, the sensational brand of preaching coming from a Reformed minister became more and more disturbing to local leaders in Dr. DeHaan's denomination, the Reformed Church in America. While a few Reformed pastors did hold views similar to DeHaan's, they were quieter about it. But most Reformed pastors and denominational theologians in the area differed sharply with DeHaan on his premillennial position. Though they seldom preached on the subject, to them the millennium would not be a literal thousand-year reign of Christ on earth, as DeHaan believed Revelation 20 states. Some believed the millennium should be thought of as the present state of the righteous in heaven; others interpreted it as being the peace enjoyed by Christians on earth; and still others thought it represented the entire period from the cross, when Satan was defeated, until the return of Christ. Whatever their varying views on the millennium, these amillennialists held that the return of the Lord from heaven would result in a general resurrection, judgment, and then eternity. Not one to hide his feelings, M. R. DeHaan let it be known that he regarded this kind of Bible teaching that spiritualizes Scripture rather than taking it for what it says as a "cancerous curse."

However, it was his views on another subject—infant baptism—that brought the outspoken pastor to the breaking point with his denomination. It all began rather quietly behind the scenes as Dr. DeHaan began comparing Reformed doctrine on baptism with other views, and with what he felt the Bible taught on the subject. Reformed or covenant theology, he observed, declares that in what is called "the church age," infant baptism replaces infant circumcision. Since, according to Reformed doctrine, the church is the Israel of the New Testament, God's covenant community is expected faithfully to present their children for baptism so that they can be "true children of the Abrahamic covenant" (Genesis 12, 13, 15, and 17) and heirs of the promise of God's blessings.

DeHaan visited several of his Reformed colleagues to discuss the matter. "I can't find anything in the Bible that comes close to suggesting that I should baptize infants," he asserted. When some of the men indicated that it was primarily a dedication, M. R. DeHaan countered, "Then why use water?"

The matter became more serious when Dr. DeHaan ignored the Reformed church calendar and did not preach on infant baptism when the subject was scheduled to be discussed from the pulpit. Church officers mentioned the matter to him, but did not seem unduly alarmed; the calendar wasn't compulsory, although pastors usually followed it.

Then one day a couple asked Dr. DeHaan to baptize their baby. He told them that his views on baptism had changed, and that he could not in good conscience do so. In later years he was to write what he, in essence, told the couple:

> The Bible does not contain anything whatsoever concerning this subject. There is no record in the Bible where babies were ever baptized, much less sprinkled. . . . God promises in His Word that if we will "train up a child in the way he should go, when he is old he will not depart from it" (Proverbs 22:6). We have a right to claim God's promises for

our children, but they certainly are not saved because they are born of Christian parents, or because they have been sprinkled as babies, nor are they covenant children; but they must come to a personal knowledge and acceptance of the Lord Jesus Christ as their own personal Savior.

Commenting further on the matter, Dr. DeHaan declared:

I believe that all children who die before the age of account-ability are saved, since they have never had the opportunity of rejecting the gospel of the Lord Jesus Christ or the light that God has given to them. We believe that Jesus died on the cross of Calvary for the sins of mankind, and today only one sin can condemn a man, and that is the sin of willfully rejecting the message that God gives to fallen man. I believe with all my heart that every baby that dies, whether before birth or after birth, before it reaches the age of accountabil-ity, goes to heaven.

With the matter of infant baptism in the open, he met with his church consistory to explain his position. He explained that he had studied the subject at length, looking both into the Bible and into writings of many theologians, and had prayed much about the matter. He simply could not see that baptism of in-fants had taken the place of circumcision. He believed only in believer's baptism, speaking of one's personal relationship to Jesus Christ and symbolizing the believer's death and resurrec-tion with Christ.

Though many of the men of the Calvary Reformed Church consistory sided with Dr. DeHaan and his non-Reformed views on the matter (17 out of 24), the announcement proved a bombshell, especially after the pastor shared his beliefs with the entire congregation on Sunday morning.

At this point, Dr. M. R. DeHaan had gone too far, said the Grand Rapids Classis of the Reformed Church in America. And on February 26, 1929, a set of six charges against Dr. DeHaan was signed and filed by nine men of one of the churches of the Classis. The charges were shortly thereafter published in a local newspaper.

As the ecclesiastical wheels ground toward an official censure, M. R. DeHaan sensed that his days within the Reformed Church were numbered.

CHAPTER 7

A Thriving New Church

"And the word of the Lord was published throughout all the region."
ACTS 13:49

Although most members of the congregation had known that a break was coming, the official announcement was made on Sunday, March 3, 1929, at the morning service of Calvary Reformed Church. Parishioners filled the sanctuary early, expectantly awaiting their pastor's comments on the brief announcement that appeared in the church bulletin: seventeen members of the consistory, their names listed, had resigned. A hush fell over the congregation as Dr. DeHaan began his announcements.

"You have read in the bulletin the notice concerning the resignation of seventeen members of the consistory," he began in his full deep voice. "These men have not only resigned from Calvary Reformed Church but also from the Reformed Church in America. They have organized a new church, which will be known as the Calvary Undenominational Church. These men comprise the new board. They have called me to be pastor of the new church and I have accepted. Beginning Wednesday evening of this coming week we will hold our first service in the building formerly occupied by the Orpheum Theatre on lower Monroe Avenue."

A twenty-inch account the next day in the *Grand Rapids Press* spelled out details of this newest development in the dramatic story of the outspoken pastor and his seventeen consistorymen. Asked by the *Press* writer if he considered that the step removed him and his consistory from the jurisdiction of the Reformed Church, Dr. DeHaan answered, "Absolutely." When the reporter suggested that the position of the Classis might be contrary to his, DeHaan asserted, "The consistory and I are out of the Reformed denomination."

In his account of the ensuing consequences, Thomas Boslooper wrote:

> A Special Session of Classis was set for March 14 at the Seventh Reformed Church when Classis was to hear the charges and DeHaan was to be confronted with them. DeHaan, however, did not appear. Another meeting was then called for April 2 at which time neither DeHaan nor an Elder from Calvary Reformed appeared. Classis did proceed with presentation of, and action on, the charges. . . . DeHaan explained that he did not appear at either session of Classis because he had resigned and considered himself no longer under the jurisdiction of the Classis. . . . Classis went ahead with the trial without DeHaan. Although Classis reported to the press that the 37 members of the Classis voted unanimously against DeHaan on all charges, the record of Classis indicated that divided votes were counted on three of the six charges and unanimous votes were cast for three of the six charges. M. R. DeHaan was found guilty of all charges

and deposed from the ministry of the Reformed Church in America as of April 2, 1929.[1]

Despite some harsh criticism from both sides, as the case of the Reformed Church in America vs. M. R. DeHaan came to a conclusion, and as he began his ministry as pastor of Calvary Undenominational Church, Dr. DeHaan spoke with love toward those with whom he so sharply differed. "I love them and know them to be sincere and honest. I still love the Reformed Church. I shall continue to love her. I shall pray for her that God may bless her. I cannot agree in all things with the brethren, but even after I am out I shall stand ready to aid and assist in any way I can in the spiritual welfare of the organization. I have no personal grievance against any individual. I believe they are wrong but I will love them as brethren."

However, the effect of Dr. DeHaan's leaving on Calvary Reformed Church was nearly catastrophic. Within a few weeks, a congregation that had numbered close to a thousand had dwindled to less than a hundred. For some time, stories appeared in the Grand Rapids newspapers with versions of the event from both sides, resulting in years of hard feelings on the part of many.

✳   ✳   ✳

The first midweek meeting of Calvary Undenominational Church on March 6, 1929, attracted a large number of people who had followed Dr. DeHaan from Calvary Reformed Church, all but filling the auditorium of the Orpheum Theatre building. And on Sunday morning, March 10, the building was filled to

---

1. Boslooper, *Grace and Glory Days*, 7–8.

capacity with 1,100 people. Such enthusiasm was to continue, due largely to the preaching and teaching of Dr. DeHaan.

The first service was graphically described by Grand Rapids upholstery dealer Lewis Steenwyk, then twenty-one and present at the service with his father and mother:

> Dr. DeHaan preached on what will take place on the earth after the rapture of the church. And, of course, he had people thumbing through their Bibles, looking up this reference, then that reference. My dad sat there and looked up the passages, and held the Bible right under my nose so I could read them too. Though I'm not emotionally inclined, I was really shook up. I had a struggle within. I knew what a lost sinner I was, and I was just simply miserable.
>
> When the invitation was given, I said to myself, "If these other people want to make fools of themselves and raise their hands and go forward in a meeting, let them do it. I'm not going to make a fool of myself." So I sat there. During the course of the invitation, it seemed to me as if someone up in the balcony above us reached down and lifted my hand, against my stubborn will. When Dr. DeHaan saw it, he said, "God bless you, young man." Just that quickly the tension was gone and there was peace. I went forward.
>
> After the service Dr. DeHaan opened the Bible with me and read Romans 10:9 and 10: "If thou shalt confess with thy mouth the Lord Jesus, and shalt believe in thine heart that God hath raised Him from the dead, thou shalt be saved. For with the heart man believeth unto righteousness; and with the mouth confession is made unto salvation." Surely I believed that and that was it. So I owe Dr. DeHaan a great debt of gratitude for leading me to the Lord Jesus Christ.

Lewis Steenwyk also recalled many memorable details of the first years at Calvary Undenominational Church:

We transferred the radio facilities from the Reformed Church to the theater and continued on the air. The 6-and-¾-hour broadcasts on radio every Sunday had a tremendous listening audience. Between the Mel Trotter Mission (with its teaching on the second coming of Christ) and Calvary Undenominational (with the speakers[2] that Dr. DeHaan brought there and his messages on the premillennial return of the Lord), we had a revival here in Grand Rapids. Tremendous! We didn't call it that; we didn't know what a revival was—the word was new to many of us. But the church was packed Sunday morning and night. People were being saved all over. Street meetings were being held. Our young people's group thought nothing of having 150–200 out on Monday night for a Bible class with Dr. DeHaan as teacher. The main youth activities centered around the Monday Bible Class, a street meeting on Tuesday evenings in the inner, poorer section of the city, prayer meeting on Wednesday, and a Saturday night street meeting. Many of those young people are today full-time ministers for the Lord.

Our Sunday evening services at Calvary Church began at 6:45 with a song service, and we did not have much special music. Dr. DeHaan kept it down to a minimum. He was a long-winded preacher, and many times would still be going at 9:15. When he gave the salvation invitation, it was not at all unusual to see people come down the aisles and go to

---

2. Among them: Dr. Arno C. Gaebelein, Dr. William L. Pettingill, Dr. Donald Grey Barnhouse, Dr. Albert Hughes, Dr. L. Sale-Harrison, Dr. Norman B. Harrison, Dr. Louis Talbot, and Dr. William McCarrell.

the prayer rooms, where personal workers counseled with them.

I believe that Dr. DeHaan's success and his power as a preacher were based on his acceptance of the Word of God as verbally inspired. He did not believe in spiritualizing the Scriptures. He believed in taking the Bible literally.

A verse that was strong with Dr. DeHaan was 2 Timothy 2:15. He believed in "rightly dividing the word of truth," as the verse says. I can remember him saying many times that there are three classes of people—Jews, Gentiles, and the church of God. When unbelieving Jews become believers, they become members of the church, Dr. DeHaan pointed out. When unbelieving Gentiles become believers they too become members of the church. So there are three groups. Dr. DeHaan urged us to read the Bible and consider to whom the Holy Spirit is speaking. Unbelieving Gentiles in the Old Testament? Unbelieving Jews? Or is it written to the church, the body of believers? If you follow that line, that method of interpretation, Dr. DeHaan pointed out, you'll not be calling the church *Israel*.

He didn't believe in accepting the blessings of Israel and forgetting the curses, as he had learned in the Reformed Church. They believe the church is spiritual Israel. Well, Dr. DeHaan used to say if we are under the Abrahamic covenant, as they believe, then we had better start over to Palestine and get our share of the Promised Land, as God promised Abraham that to his seed He would give all this land "from the river of Egypt unto the great river Euphrates for an everlasting possession."

✻   ✻   ✻

Reitze and Johanna DeHaan with sons John, Ralph, and baby Martin

Martin DeHaan,
high school graduation

Dr. Martin DeHaan,
graduation, University of Illinois Medical School

*Dr. and Mrs. DeHaan
and Ruth*

The Rev. M. R. DeHaan

The DeHaan home in Byron Center, Michigan

Offices of Radio Bible Class, Michigan Street, Grand Rapids, Michigan

*In the broadcast studio, left to right: Marvin DeHaan, M.R., Richard DeHaan,
A. Haaksma, E. and S. Oppenhuizen, and J. Brom*

The DeHaan home on Leonard Street,
where they lived for many years

Richard W. DeHaan

"Happiness is a fishing boat and a good catch"

Radio Bible Class office on Kalamazoo Avenue

The lithograph department prepares labels for mailing Class materials

Dr. DeHaan leads a weekly chapel for the Radio Bible Class staff

Left to right: Leona Hertel, Henry Bosch, Clair Hess, and M.R. in the studio

M.R. used the blackboard effectively

Priscilla and M.R. in the office

Left to right: Richard DeHaan, A. Haaksma, G. Bergsma, H. Bosch, S. Oppenhuizen, S. Noordyk

*Henry G. Bosch,
the first editor of* Our Daily Bread

*M.R. and Priscilla celebrate
their 46th wedding anniversary*

The "Rest-a-While" cabin where M.R. enjoyed spending time

Dr. DeHaan and Rev. Yutaka Akichika
The map shows all the radio stations broadcasting Radio Bible Class at the time

M.R. in his characteristic teaching pose

A well-known photo of Dr. DeHaan,
used in his books and Radio Bible Class materials

Calvary Undenominational met in the old Orpheum Theatre building until the summer of 1929, then moved to the St. Cecilia building, pending the completion of a new building. On January 26, 1930, the congregation of some seven hundred members moved to its new quarters at Michigan Street and College Avenue, N.E., an impressive rambling structure boasting a new auditorium and a renovated former elementary school.

Now settled in its own building, Calvary Undenominational Church stepped up its program, attracting greater crowds than ever. The auditorium seated around 2,000, and often chairs were brought in to accommodate the overflow.

M. R. DeHaan recognized the church's radio ministry as probably the most outstanding domestic missionary work of Calvary Undenominational Church. "This work is definitely blessed in a peculiar way by God for the conversion of sinners, the edification of saints, and the comfort of the shut-ins," stated the church dedication booklet. "Our radio ministry brings to an unseen audience four services each Lord's Day. At 10 o'clock in the morning we broadcast our regular Sunday morning worship. At 2 in the afternoon we present the radio request program. At 6:45 in the evening, our regular evening evangelistic service, and at 10 at night, a good-night hour of fellowship and heart-to-heart talk."

Dr. DeHaan "gave the Word like medicine," as some termed it, recalling his years as a practicing physician. To the embarrassment of some and the amusement of others, he sometimes pounded the pulpit vigorously and, in his enthusiasm, threw a leg over it Billy Sunday style.

In making his sermons relevant to the times, Dr. DeHaan borrowed ideas from editorial columns of newspapers. When the *Grand Rapids Herald* posed the question, "What is wrong with our educational system?" the Calvary pastor fired back from the pulpit with the sure remedy: "It ignores the missing link. The editor says, 'Somewhere in our educational system is a weak link.' Ah, no, not a weak one, but a missing one! No system—economic, political, or educational—can prosper that ignores the sovereignty of God's will and the existence of One who will judge all things by His Son, Jesus Christ."

In his message Dr. DeHaan took sharp issue with Leslie A. Butler, superintendent of the Grand Rapids Public Schools, who had declared that "as education increases, crime decreases." Butler quoted statistics showing that 90 percent of the inmates of a Michigan prison never received an education above the sixth grade. "Such jumping at conclusions," said DeHaan,

> alarms us, especially when it comes from an educator like Mr. Butler. There is no foundation for the statement that "as education increases, crime decreases." The reverse is true. During the past fifteen years, education has gone ahead by leaps and bounds, and crime has kept up at a commensurate pace. . . . Education has done nothing to retard the unwavering increase of wickedness in the human heart. . . . We attack man in the wrong place; the trouble is with the heart and not the head.
>
> There was a time not so many years ago when, in the school system of this land, God was recognized and the Bible was revered and taught. They were days of God's blessing on this fair land. But gradually the devil plied his trade until God has been thrust out of the schools and the Bible either banished or put alongside of any other secular book for the study of literature or history. . . . Putting the Bible back in school is the cure for educational problems!

Like Peter of old, M. R. DeHaan preached with great power and people were "cut to the heart" (Acts 2:37). But he was just as interested in talking to one or two persons as to a crowd. He always had time for people and kept in contact with old friends. When he learned that his driver from his doctoring days, Maynard Vander Zaag, had had a son, he visited the Vander Zaag home. "He's certainly a fine boy. Let's give him back to the Lord," said Dr. DeHaan, and he proceeded to pray a dedicatory prayer for the child. The Vander Zaags firmly believed that God answered that prayer, for their son Bob gave himself to the Lord's service and became a pastor.

His concern for families was evident at weddings when Dr. DeHaan would exhort couples at length on the need for making Christ the center of their home and teaching their children to follow in the ways of God. "He exhorted us at our wedding," Lewis Steenwyk pointed out, "and, as I recall it, he laid special emphasis on going to the Lord with our problems."

※　※　※

In the late 1930s, Calvary Undenominational Church members began whispering about problems within the church. Trouble broke openly one day in May 1938 when Dr. DeHaan returned from a week's meetings in another city and discovered that three men on the board, who also comprised the music committee, had fired Floyd D. Leary, the director of music and young people's work. Displeased with this action, Dr. DeHaan, in clear, well-chosen terms, tongue-lashed the offending board members. On Sunday, May 15, he called a special congregational meeting for the following Tuesday, at which time he exhorted the membership to give Leary a vote of confidence, which they did. Leary, who had offered to resign, agreed to continue serving.

Tension and disagreement between Dr. DeHaan and the Calvary Undenominational Church board had been building for some time, however. Dr. DeHaan wanted a certain amount of autonomy and authority on matters pertaining to the church and his ministry. And given his strong and decisive personality, it is understandable that he had trouble working for consensus with a group of board members.

Now, infuriated over the dismissal of Leary, Dr. DeHaan asked the congregation to declare the recent election of deacons and elders void. A majority voted in favor of his request and gave him authority to appoint a committee to replace the board until the next annual meeting in March 1939. As a result, six men, five of them ex-members, took legal action by obtaining an injunction on Dr. DeHaan and the committee of five he had appointed to conduct church business. It was served on Friday, May 20.

The following Sunday, May 22, Dr. DeHaan resigned. On Monday he was quoted by the *Grand Rapids Herald* as resigning for two reasons: health and conscience. "I have conscientious scruples about going to law about a church matter, and because of these scruples and the condition of my health, I have resigned. I have no plans at present, except to regain my health if possible."

Indeed, Dr. DeHaan had been ill for much of the spring and had been absent from the pulpit for all but two of sixteen Sundays. Dr. DeHaan's son Richard, then fifteen, years later recalled these trying days in a series of radio messages on "Men Sent from God":

I do rejoice in recounting those happy seasons of revival blessing [at Calvary Undenominational Church]; however, there are some things I wish I could forget: events which have made an indelible mark and impression upon my life and which loom up before me today as a terrible nightmare. Oh, that I could erase them from my mind forever. For while the work of a pastor can be most satisfying and rewarding, it also involves extremely difficult, trying, discouraging, and disappointing experiences. The misunderstandings, the false accusations, and the opposition, especially from those within the church, can sap the energy, break the spirit, and frustrate the efforts of even the most dedicated servant.

Even now, I can visualize my dad slumped down in a chair sobbing out his heart to God. I can still feel the quickening of my own pulse as time after time he found it necessary to excuse himself from the evening meals due to nervous exhaustion. How his countenance changed during those days of adversity and difficulty. He began to stoop under the heavy load until almost broken in spirit, and physically exhausted, his weary heart rebelled. Arriving home from school one day, I saw him lying on the davenport, his face contorted, spelling out the severe pain in his chest, brought on by the tension, the extreme burdens and pressures of a conscientious ministry.

From his sickbed, Dr. DeHaan, writing for the April 10, 1938, church bulletin, blamed his illness on "multitudinous cares and responsibilities of the work of the church, spiritual, financial, missionary, radio and local." He urged the congregation to pray for him and be faithful "in regard to these matters. These are stressing days," he continued. "A great recession is on. But to God's people a recession is a challenge—not a signal to lie down."

Now, following his bombshell of May 22, 1938, he was not only a depressed, sick man—he was a pastor without a job.[2]

Paul and Barnabas had clashed and separated over John Mark in the matter of his joining their missionary team; Dr. M. R. DeHaan had clashed with brethren and "departed asunder one from the other." Paul chose Silas, and Barnabas selected Mark, and the Holy Spirit used both teams; likewise, God chose to continue blessing Calvary Undenominational Church, and He had a great worldwide ministry ahead for M. R. DeHaan.

---

2. Some years later, a Calvary Undenominational Church committee sought to bring about a peaceful settlement of the matter. This resulted in renewed fellowship, and Dr. DeHaan subsequently preached from the Calvary pulpit in a guest role.

CHAPTER 8

A 50-WATT BEGINNING

"Behold, I have set before thee an open door, and no man can shut it:
for thou hast a little strength, and hast kept my word, and hast
not denied my name."
REVELATION 3:8

A short while after he left the pulpit of Calvary
Undenominational Church, Dr. DeHaan met for lunch in
Detroit with his friend Dr. Billy McCarrell, the Illinois pastor
whose Bible classes DeHaan had attended in Grand Rapids. "I
really got a good sock on the schnozzle," he told McCarrell as
he recounted the events leading to his resignation.

McCarrell, in Detroit to teach a Bible class, leaned forward
and looked DeHaan squarely in the eye. "Doctor," he said,
"God has given you a great gift in Bible teaching. Perhaps He is
opening the door to a new type of ministry for you."

Even while struggling to regain his health that year, Dr.
DeHaan taught several weekday Bible classes, sometimes showing up to teach when the average person might have stayed
home in bed. On Monday nights he conducted a class in Flint,
Michigan; on Tuesday nights, Buffalo, New York; on Thursday
nights, Grand Rapids; on Friday nights, Detroit, Michigan; and

87

on Saturday nights, East Detroit. His popularity became more
and more widespread, and thousands tuned in to hear him on
the Michigan Radio Network. He taught with authority, making the way of salvation through God's grace plain, and exciting spiritual pulses with lessons on prophecy. As a result, it was
common to find more than 1,000 persons at many of the weekday sessions.

Little did Billy McCarrell know how prophetic his words
were the day he suggested that perhaps God had a new kind of
Bible-teaching ministry for M. R. DeHaan. And certainly Dr.
DeHaan had no inkling that the Sunday morning, September
4, 1938, he broadcast live for the first time on radio station
WEXL, a 50-watt outlet in Royal Oak, a Detroit suburb, would
mark the beginning of a Bible-teaching radio ministry that
would reach around the world.

That first radio program was called *The Detroit Bible Class*
and the format of the half-hour broadcast was simple. Dr.
DeHaan taught the day's lesson, and Elmer and Maynard
Oppenhuizen, brothers whom Dr. DeHaan imported from
Grand Rapids, opened and closed the broadcast singing "Tell
Me the Story of Jesus." Later, in 1939, the Doctor asked Henry
Bosch, a baritone who was on radio himself in Grand Rapids,
to join the Oppenhuizen brothers. Occasionally Dr. DeHaan,
with the informality characteristic of those early broadcasts,
would join the trio and make it a quartet by adding his raspy
bass.

In the early years there was no rehearsal in the studio. A
Salvation Army Band played a concert immediately preceding
the DeHaan broadcast, and as the station announcer made the
station break, the bandsmen raced out of the studio and the
DeHaan team hurried in, all within the space of a minute. Mrs.

Elmer Oppenhuizen would hardly be seated at the organ when the red light came on signaling the trio to begin singing.

Often several members of the DeHaan family accompanied the Doctor to the station. Recollections of those early days were later somewhat hazy, but Richard recalled that the entire family was thrilled at the response to the program. One staff member remembered young Richard and Marvin leaning from a window in the radio studios high above the Detroit River, trying to spit on objects below and sailing paper airplanes. But the mischievous boys were soon pitching in more and more as the program grew.

❈   ❈   ❈

Now fully convinced that God had indeed called him to a career in gospel broadcasting, in 1941 Dr. M. R. DeHaan set up headquarters in Grand Rapids. At this point he changed the name from *The Detroit Bible Class* to *Radio Bible Class* to more accurately reflect the growing reach of the broadcast. The program became even more widely known after it originated from CKLW, a 50,000-watt super-station in Windsor/Detroit.

When Dr. DeHaan began to organize Radio Bible Class in Grand Rapids, he hired Leona Hertel, daughter of a close friend of Priscilla's, to be his secretary. Priscilla also helped in the office, which was in their home. "I remember very well the day we had $85.00 in the bank to pay bills," she said. "It was a big day."

It was with great enthusiasm that Dr. DeHaan picked up the mail when he was home. Old-time employees tell of his delight in doing so, whistling, joking, talking, and thanking God for the means to continue broadcasting. His confidence that God's hand was on him in the radio ministry not only strengthened his faith but proved good therapy for his body, and his health steadily improved, enabling him to work long hours and fill an increasing number of preaching and teaching engagements.

Meanwhile, sons Richard and Marvin were pitching in more and more as the work increased, running a printing press in the basement, doing janitorial work, and licking stamps. Both boys, blessed with deep voices like their father's, also got their chances to help with the broadcast itself. When Richard was about eighteen, he did the opening announcement, offered the sermon booklet, and closed the program. Marvin announced for the first time when he was fifteen, subbing for the absent Richard, and continued to do so when he was needed, until he became too involved with his own studies in medical school.

From the beginning on 50-watt WEXL, the Doctor published sermon booklets, including in them the radio messages.

One day in 1956, in the studio, Henry Bosch, one of the singers on the broadcast, suggested that listeners needed something to read on a daily basis to complement the weekly radio ministry and monthly sermon booklets. Dr. DeHaan readily agreed, and plans were soon underway to produce a daily devotional booklet. Bosch served as the first editor of the publication, and Richard DeHaan suggested that it be called *Our Daily Bread*. The name seemed to fit both the practical and spiritual purpose for which the devotional was created.

The printing of the sermon booklets and the devotional guides, plus radio time, required regular financial support, but from the moment Dr. DeHaan founded Radio Bible Class, he trusted God to set the pace of growth, choosing not to seek support over the airwaves. Though he occasionally made financial needs known in newsletters, he vowed that he would not let needs "get in the way" of the message, nor use proceeds to develop an elaborate superstructure.

Dr. DeHaan, full of both faith and conservative good sense, often said, "If the Lord wants us to go ahead, He'll supply the money. If He doesn't send it in, that'll be our signal to quit broadcasting."

If a new staff member suggested that gimmicks be employed to step up contributions, he was immediately squelched. "We'll never use come-ons like sand from Palestine or rain water that fell into the Jordan," the Doctor said more than once. Instead, he depended on God to "incline the hearts of Thy people to send the money."

❋   ❋   ❋

Dr. M. R. DeHaan considered his "class members," as he called those who faithfully listened to and supported the broadcast and received the literature, the finest people in the world. Sensing their prayers as he ministered, he often spoke in these terms: "We thank God for the thousands of you dear saints of God who intercede for us in our work of broadcasting the gospel. Praying is, after all, the greatest thing you can do for us. I am convinced that if it were not for you, the unseen host of unnoticed pray-ers, the devil would have had the program of the *Radio Bible Class* off the air long ago."

Dr. DeHaan himself prayed fervently for the ministry God had given him. Then, both figuratively and sometimes literally, he rolled up his sleeves and expounded the Word till perspiration poured from his body.

For him, there was nothing more thrilling than to lean forward before a microphone and expound the wonders of the Bible. Whether taping a message or teaching on a live broadcast, he taught almost as if he could see his vast audience, occasionally interjecting such comments as, "I'll repeat that Bible reference—I think someone missed it." He thought of his listeners as taking notes and thumbing through their Bibles with him as he taught.

While there were some who did not appreciate his gravelly voice, regular listeners considered it an asset. And despite its raspiness, his voice had a certain mellowness. But above all he spoke with conviction that left the impression that M. R. DeHaan had just come from a private audience with God.

"The Lord used that voice with its distinctive quality to be sort of a trademark," his son Richard said. "When folks once heard it, there was no mistaking it when they ran across it again on the dial. After a few words, there was no doubt: 'That's the man.' The Lord used his voice. In fact, some have written since his home-going that they miss the 'sweetest voice in radio!'"

"At one time, the Doctor had a voice somewhat like Richard's—deep and mellow and mild," recalled Priscilla. "But in the early days of his evangelistic fervor, he preached in tent meetings and at other gatherings without the aid of public-address systems, and it was very hard on his voice."

Son Marvin, speaking as a physician, speculated that in those early days his father's voice developed its gruff qualities from chronic laryngitis. The vocal cords became inflamed and the constant irritation caused the cords to thicken.

"It never really bothered him particularly," Marvin said, thinking back to the beginning years of Radio Bible Class. "He would complain when he would lose his voice or when it would be very poor. He used to gargle a lot with hot salt water. And I mean hot—he never did anything halfway. Whatever you do, do it right, was his philosophy."

Then, in the summer of 1946, the distinctive voice was suddenly silenced. While doing a live radio program, Dr. DeHaan was suddenly struck by pain in his chest and arms. His voice faltered, but likely few listeners noticed. With beads of perspiration on his forehead and with his face gripped in pain, he finished the broadcast. Staff workers rushed to him and a doctor was called.

M. R. DeHaan had suffered a severe heart attack. For months to come, his voice would be missing from the airwaves.

CHAPTER 9

A WORLDWIDE MINISTRY

"Go ye into all the world, and preach the gospel to every creature."
MARK 16:15

When Dr. DeHaan had his heart attack and was out of action for several months, there was one bright side for the ministry: his broadcast would continue uninterrupted, for he had a stand-in in the person and voice of his tall, twenty-three-year-old son Richard.

With a desire to become a minister, Richard had entered Northern Baptist Seminary in Chicago in 1944, after attending Calvin College in Grand Rapids and doing further work at Wheaton College near Chicago. Richard had been attending classes four days a week at the seminary in Chicago, then working with his father on Saturdays, Sundays, and Mondays. It was no secret that Dr. DeHaan was grooming him for the day when he would fill in as teacher, with the plan of his someday taking over the broadcast. Thus, when Richard stepped in for his ailing father, the Doctor thanked God for his willing substitute.

Richard filled in until his father was strong enough to again take his place at the microphone. On the first broadcast M.R. made after his heart attack, he spoke from his bed at home.

With his voice emotion-filled and trembling, he thanked his listening audience for their prayers, and for the way they had stood by the Class during his recovery.

The radio program was the backbone of the DeHaan ministry, and it was here that M.R. was in his element, whether broadcasting or speaking with conviction to make a point to an associate regarding the wisdom of adding certain stations or dropping others. He periodically spent hours reviewing the radio log, culling out the weaker stations and seeking better time spots. He believed in spending Radio Bible Class dollars as wisely as possible, reaching the most people at the least expense. And as Dr. DeHaan and his staff prayed, they saw doors of air time continue to open. In time, the broadcast was reaching millions through hundreds of strategically located stations across the U.S., Canada, and in many foreign lands.

Because of DeHaan's successful formula, other broadcasters journeyed to Grand Rapids to learn from him. They recognized him not only as an able Bible teacher but also as an astute businessman. "How do you handle your mail so efficiently?" "How do you carry on a printing operation and send out so much literature with so few people?" They asked these and many other questions.

As Dr. DeHaan showed them the Radio Bible Class operation, one of the answers became clear. They saw that, in his wisdom, he had surrounded himself with capable people. Visitors chatting with veteran employees such as Henry Bosch would have heard: "Dr. DeHaan hires consecrated people and has kept a good spirit going. He has always said, 'Remember, this is not primarily a business; this is a ministry! We must be businesslike, to be sure, but it's first of all a ministry.' He has taught us to do things 'as unto the Lord.'"

✳ ✳ ✳

Though the Doctor's gruff exterior could be intimidating to employees, they soon found his door and heart wide open to them. One young woman, a part-time worker, came to him to seek counsel regarding her career. Should she continue with school or go to work immediately in the Lord's service? He strongly advised her to prepare herself and not follow her emotions.

He shared bits of humor with the staff as he walked about the office, his hands in his back pockets. He enjoyed theological discussions with the men at coffee break, sometimes giving a ten-minute Bible message while drinking extra strong coffee so hot that the fellows "thought steam would come out his ears," as one man put it.

Whenever the Doctor was in town, he met with the office staff for their regular morning chapel services. Often he shared messages he planned to use on the broadcast. And he periodically reminded employees that they were rendering a service to the Lord—that they were, in a real sense, missionaries. "When you think of missions, think of the Radio Bible Class," he urged.

In serious discussions with executives, Dr. DeHaan exhibited his strong convictions. If he believed something, he came right to the point. Tact was not his strongest virtue, and in earlier years, especially, he might crash his fist into his hand, or onto a desk, to punctuate his remarks. There were times when he was more like Simon than Peter. "I don't care! I want it done this way," he'd storm.

One close associate said that in later years his manner did soften or mellow somewhat. And when he did react harshly, "It would be only a little while and Doc would come out and say,

'I'm sorry; I don't know why I did that. I shouldn't have told you in that way. I should have been more kind.'"

✻　✻　✻

In early 1958, Radio Bible Class passed an important milestone in the ministry when the Doctor dedicated to the Lord's service a new efficiently designed building. Conditions in the old windowless ex-theater building where they had been headquartered had become hopelessly overcrowded, forcing the conservative Doctor to build. For the first time both he and Richard had separate offices they could call their own.

Dr. DeHaan would walk about the sparkling, cheerful new working area and say to an associate, "This thing is scaring me more than ever. I never envisioned this. I don't know why God ever picked me."

But every mail delivery brought evidence that the Doctor's vigorous teaching was making an impact around the world. Besides the letters of thanks, there were the letters of "no thanks." Even those filled with hate and scorn brought a certain satisfaction. They usually amused the Doctor and gave him assurance that he was among the blessed of Luke 6:22, hated and reproached for the Lord's sake.

"You know, when you throw a stone at a pack of dogs, the one that howls the loudest is the one that got hit," he philosophized. "I always feel that when they are howling I must have done something worthwhile. I must have hit them with the truth. When I preach, I like to see people really become concerned, repent, and get saved. However, when I see some getting angry, I realize that this is also bound to happen. It's the opposite side of the two-edged sword of the Word."

When, in his opinion, writers were really serious in their inquiries, he replied, usually within twenty-four hours. But when letters contained clever catch questions and traps, he utterly ignored them. "There are so many people from whom we never hear a word unless they have a gripe or an argument, or something to criticize," he once said. "For these we keep a special file which we call the 'round file.' How I thank God for wastebaskets. What a labor-saving device they have proven to be. There are so many important things for the Christian to do that he cannot afford to waste time in unprofitable activities, arguments, debates, and discussions."

In the early years of Radio Bible Class, Dr. DeHaan believed he could answer any theological question that was asked him about the Bible. In later years his attitude changed. "I must admit that my ignorance of the Bible is most appalling," he wrote. "Over and over and over again I must tell people, 'My honest answer is: I don't know!' Sometimes I say, 'The best I can do is refer you to Deuteronomy 29:29—"The secret things belong unto the Lord our God. . . ."'"

Although he had his opportunities, M. R. DeHaan never accepted any honorary degrees, preferring to keep only his earned M.D. after his name. He kept up on medical advances to some degree through discussions with his physician son, Marvin, and by reading medical literature that continued coming to him. He also offered certain medical advice in some of his writings and occasionally in messages, and thus in a loose sense he was still a practicing physician.

In his book *Broken Things*, he wrote sagaciously concerning the relationship of physical disease to mental and spiritual health, and he occasionally gave bits of medical advice in his *Our Daily Bread* articles. For example, he lambasted "home remedies, worthless nostrums, cure-alls, diets, vitamins, minerals, salves, [and] greases," making "the average medicine cabinet look like a miniature drugstore," he asserted. "Throw away 95% of those pills and gadgets . . . eat normal, balanced diets, quit worrying about . . . health, go to bed on time, and be more concerned with . . . spiritual health than the physical . . . [and] live longer and happier!"

At the office Dr. DeHaan occasionally examined employees' sore throats, rashes, and other ailments. Once when Asian flu threatened Grand Rapids, he came to the office with his medical kit and gave all RBC employees a vaccine, resulting in only a minimum of absenteeism because of the disease.

Occasionally when the call came, "Is there a doctor in the house?" he hurried to meet the emergency. Once while participating in an all-day church conference, he was interrupted in the midst of a sermon with the summons, "Quick! Come downstairs. A woman is dying!" Excusing himself, he left the pulpit and went to aid the victim. She had been helping prepare a meal and had sampled a piece of chicken, which became lodged in her throat. The woman was on her back and unconscious when Doctor arrived.

"I remembered what they had told me in medical school—in an emergency use emergency measures," Dr. DeHaan told an associate later. "So, because I had no instruments or anything, I put my fingers down her throat, tearing the tissue some because my fingers were too short for the job. I grabbed the piece of meat, then gave her resuscitation, and brought her back. She had an awfully sore throat because of it, but it saved her life."

Although he relished his occasional role of practicing physician, he often averred that he was not sorry he had left his medical career to preach the gospel. Being God's obstetrician in thousands of spiritual births brought him even greater joy than delivering babies as a country doctor. And there were countless testimonies of encouragement to the ministry.

One man who heard Dr. DeHaan's broadcast later wrote: "Your message did something nothing else has ever done. I was drinking wine and beer in my room, and I heard that song, 'Do You Know Jesus?' and a memory came to me about Grand Rapids where I was born. I am a retired switchman. When I heard you I said, 'Well, here goes the works.' I knelt beside my bed and asked God to take me. I got up, got my wine and beer, and poured it down the drain. I ate my breakfast and prayed again. Doctor, pray for me. Please send me some books to help me live for God."

A Roman Catholic who had incurred the wrath of her church for marrying a divorced Protestant wrote Dr. DeHaan to tell him that his book *Revelation* had been instrumental in a great change in their spiritual lives. Her husband's pastor had given him the book, and he was restored to fellowship with the Lord through it, and she had committed her life to Christ. "We want to live for the Lord and hear all we can about His Word," she continued. "Thank you for the help your broadcasts and booklets have been to us."

Dr. Donald Johns, a Grand Rapids pediatrician, once gladdened the heart of Dr. DeHaan with the story related to him by a young father who, with his wife, had brought their baby in to him for treatment. Having discovered some Radio Bible Class booklets in the waiting room, the father said:

> Dr. DeHaan's ministry has had a real effect upon our home. When I was a child my parents came home one Sunday evening from a party, quarreling and arguing, and everything was going wrong. They turned on the radio and Dr. DeHaan was bringing a message. As they listened, they realized that

this was meant for them, and at the close of the program when Dr. DeHaan urged them to settle the question of their salvation *now*, they both got on their knees in the living room before the davenport and received Christ as their own personal Savior. Their lives were changed, and our home was changed. Later on, my parents led me to the Lord, and I knelt in that same living room, before that same davenport, and asked the Lord to come into my heart and life.

On a visit to Tokyo, Dr. Johns met another man whose life was changed because of the ministry. "Last night at the crusade meeting a Japanese pastor heard me introduced as being a doctor from Michigan," Johns wrote to the Doctor, "and very excitedly he sputtered out, 'I was saved through Dr. DeHaan's ministry. He baptized me in Washington.' Through your ministry he found Jesus Christ and now pastors a fundamental, evangelistic church here in Tokyo." Dr. Johns was referring to the Rev. Yutaka Akichika, who met Christ under Dr. DeHaan's ministry in 1939. Akichika's wife was converted through a Radio Bible Class broadcast some time later.

Commenting on the Japanese couple, Dr. DeHaan once wrote that there was no greater thrill to him than to see "his children" still walking in the truth years afterward. As he wrote in the Radio Bible Class newsletter:

> There was a time early in my ministry that I often said, "The greatest joy of a Christian is to lead a soul to Christ." As the years passed, I changed my mind. . . . So many, over whom we rejoiced when they made their professions, soon fell by the wayside, and our joy came to ultimate grief and sorrow. But to come back to a place years afterward and find "converts" growing in grace, walking in the truth—this is the

greatest joy. And this is also Scriptural, for John says his greatest joy was "to hear that my children walk in truth" [3 John 4].

As I travel about the country, my greatest joy is to meet, everywhere I go, folks who testify that ten, twenty, or thirty years ago they found Christ under my preaching. What a joy to receive letters in the mail constantly, telling us how years ago they were saved listening to the radio. A missionary writes from the field: "I am here because of a sermon I heard you preach fourteen years ago, which resulted in the surrender of my life to Jesus." A pastor in Washington, while introducing me at a CBMC banquet, told how, sitting at his radio sixteen years earlier he had been saved and dedicated his life to the ministry.

A classic example of a convert continuing to walk in truth was a Jewish woman who wrote that "God was good enough to open my eyes and ears to the marvelous fact that the Messiah did come to earth and died on the cross for me." She told how a Christian friend mailed her "a pamphlet by Dr. DeHaan and informed me that her church was praying for Jews. I was astonished, for I didn't know anyone needed to pray for us," she continued. "Then I read the booklet and thought, *This isn't in my Bible.* I looked up the references and, sure enough, it was there. I started reading out of curiosity, and the more I read, the more God revealed His message to me. Every doubt and question was answered like magic. This all began ten months ago. Now my whole family has come to know Jesus. We have a Bible class in our home, and many of my bewildered Jewish friends are joining us. I listen to your broadcast on Sunday morning and receive a special blessing each time."

One of the most unusual cases on record at Radio Bible Class involved Robert Davis, an inmate at a penitentiary in Pennsylvania. In 1957 he wrote that "by chance" he had heard Dr. DeHaan on the radio and had read some of his messages. Facing the electric chair for murder, he wanted to be sure he knew the true meaning of salvation.

As soon as they received Davis's letter, Radio Bible Class sent him a letter and literature. Then, in God's providence, the Rev. Henry Broersma, a visitation minister from Calvary Undenominational Church who was visiting the Radio Bible Class office, heard about the prisoner. "Wouldn't it be worth a trip to talk to him?" he asked. This triggered a series of circumstances that took Broersma to the penitentiary. There he talked to the death row inmate, and Robert Davis indicated a trust in Jesus Christ during the counseling session. Later, Davis was granted a new trial and his death sentence was commuted to life in prison. But as he awaited trial, he witnessed to other men and at least six more declared their trust in Christ and began studying God's Word.

A sequel to the conversion of Davis came when Broersma called again at the penitentiary and asked for Davis by his number. Presently a guard brought a prisoner to him and said, "Here's your man." But it was not Robert Davis; it was a "wrong number." This man was Cleveland Thompson, he told Broersma. A conversation followed, and Thompson, the "wrong number," committed himself to Christ. Nine weeks later he walked to the electric chair, and within moments went into eternity, "absent from the body . . . present with the Lord" (2 Corinthians 5:8).

Henry Broersma helped in another unusual case involving a young man serving time in a Michigan prison for negligent homicide. The mother of the victim wrote to Radio Bible Class in early 1958 and asked that the staff pray with her for the prisoner's salvation. Gospel literature was sent and workers prayed. Later, the mother wrote:

> On the evening of February 13, Rev. Broersma called to give me the wonderful news—it had been his privilege that afternoon to lead the boy to the Lord. . . . What seems at the time like utter heartbreak to us is meant for our good, and is just part of something wonderful beyond compare that we'll understand fully in God's time. . . .
>
> We had a letter from him this week. What a change it was from all previous letters! There was calm and peace and certainty and belief in Jesus Christ registered in this one. The others had always been more or less erratic, doubtful, somewhat fearful and confused, but not this last one! On two occasions he mentioned your booklets and expressed eagerness and pleasure in reading them. . . ."

One rewarding aspect of Dr. DeHaan's ministry resulted from the fact that among listeners were many men of the clergy, from preachers with small congregations to evangelists with wide influence.

A widely known evangelist once said, "I have listened to him almost every Sunday for many years. A great deal of my Bible knowledge came from his teaching." And a Catholic priest once wrote, "For the past year or two I have been listening to you on the radio on Sunday mornings as I return from a sanatorium where I offer holy mass . . . and I think you are doing a great deal of good . . . and speak the truth . . . ."

While people deeply affected by the Radio Bible Class ministry are vast in number and are found around the world, M. R. DeHaan never kept a record of results. "God keeps the records," he often said. But knowledge of the fact that his was a fruitful ministry made him teach and preach even more vigorously, and sent him out far from Grand Rapids with the message of redeeming grace and the returning Redeemer.

CHAPTER 10

GLIMPSES OF THE DOCTOR

*"Preaching . . . and teaching those things which concern the
Lord Jesus Christ, with all confidence. . . ."*
ACTS 28:31

While M. R. DeHaan preached to millions around the world by radio, he also did considerable traveling to speak in churches and Bible conference centers. And while he loved his work before the radio microphone, something about being before a live audience stimulated him. He identified with those before him, compassion gripping him. As on the radio, he spoke with unction and authority, and his rumbling voice undoubtedly gave many the feeling they were listening to a prophet.

Seldom one to harp on fringe issues, he spoke in church services and conferences more concerning the do's of the Christian life than the don'ts, preaching that when believers let the Lord Jesus live His life through them, bad habits and sins of life fall away. To him, unbelief was the major issue. He was concerned about people "playing church," and about their need to study the Bible and believe God's promises for them, to become mighty spiritual forces in their communities. He also saw men and women on the broad road to destruction, people desperately in need of the Savior.

In services Dr. DeHaan squirmed through what he called "interminable preliminaries." He knew that certain things had to happen before he could preach, so he tolerated congregational singing, special numbers, and announcements up to a certain point. But a half-hour of preliminaries seemed sufficient; longer than that made him antsy.

When introduced, he brushed off praise, appearing to despise it. In his opening remarks, he enjoyed ribbing fellow ministers and often included other bits of humor, bringing laughter and relaxing his audience. Then suddenly he would plunge into his message in all seriousness. Cleverly, he worked in occasional illustrations, sometimes personal ones relating to his medical days or to the out-of-doors.

In his early years of preaching, M.R. prepared complete sermon manuscripts. By the midpoint of his career, he depended on one-page outlines. But in later years he used no notes at all, except for comments scrawled in the margins of his Bible. His prodigious mind, with its photographic memory and ability to produce information on a myriad of subjects, stood him in good stead. He was firm and organized in his thinking. One, two, three. People understood what he meant. He was easy to follow.

With great insight into the truths of the Bible, he sought to stimulate listeners to get into the Scriptures, to think and meditate on God's Word. One of his specialties was typology. In scores of Old Testament passages, he found pictures of the Savior. For example, he saw Joseph, not recognized by his brothers until his second appearance to them, as an illustration of Christ, who came to His own and was not received but will be recognized when they see Him again.

Although early on in his preaching M.R. moved about the platform, gesticulating vigorously, after being conditioned by being tied to a microphone in radio speaking, he remained close to the pulpit during most of his preaching years and used fewer gestures. Typically he held his Bible in one hand and gestured authoritatively with it, sometimes emphatically thumping the pulpit.

Young people, as well as seasoned Bible students, listened intently to M.R.'s profound but easy-to-grasp messages, and though he didn't wear blinking bow ties or try to speak their lingo, teenagers enjoyed talking personally with him and found him a warm person. He spoke many times at Hampden Du Bose Academy in Zellwood, Florida, as well as at other schools, and after the services students flocked around him, his bald head shining among them.

Because of his familiarity with Scripture, Dr. DeHaan could fashion a sermon to suit the occasion on short notice. Arriving in Harrisburg, Pennsylvania, for a Bible conference, he learned that his hosts had been upset by a report that he had died. Someone had produced a newspaper clipping from a Michigan paper that caused the concern. The reason for the confusion was the death of another Grand Rapids man named DeHaan. A curious crowd assembled for the conference, and mouths dropped open as the Doctor announced his text: "Revelation 1:18—'I am he that liveth, and was dead: and, behold, I am alive for evermore. . . .'" He began, "The reports you heard about my death were true; I did die, but I am now here risen from the dead, and am alive forevermore."

His explanation put his audience at ease. Revelation 1:18, he said, applies first of all to the Lord Jesus Christ but also to every Christian, who was once dead in sins (Ephesians 2:1), but through the power of Christ arose (Ephesians 2:5). "Every

Christian can say, 'I am one who lives in Christ. I have been crucified with Christ; nevertheless I live' (Galatians 2:20). Yes," he continued, "the report you heard was true, for I died, but now am alive forevermore! Praise the Lord!"

❋   ❋   ❋

Dr. DeHaan's speaking engagements often took him on extensive trips. Usually his wife, Priscilla, accompanied him, serving as chief suitcase packer and navigator with a road map.

Curiously, Dr. DeHaan, though an authority on details relating to Israel, never journeyed to the Holy Land. Half humorously, half seriously, he said, "All you do when you come back is show a lot of pictures, and you don't have time for your message." He didn't criticize his close friends and others who took groups to Bible lands. That was their business. But for himself, he was content to travel in the U.S. and Canada. Once Priscilla begged him to take her across the border into Mexico when they were in California. After they spent the night in a third-rate hotel in Mexicali, Priscilla did a bit of shopping the next morning while the Doctor reluctantly waited. And his countenance brightened when they crossed back to native soil.

In his travels, the Doctor had countless memorable adventures, meeting and chatting with people he met along the way, encountering Radio Bible Class members in unlikely places, and exploring old houses.

Figuratively, and sometimes literally, he came to a screeching stop when he spotted a dilapidated, abandoned house, somewhat to the annoyance of his wife. To Priscilla, this meant either a long wait in the car or a walk through musty rooms, up and down creaking stairways, poking into rat-infested basements. But to M.R., an old house brought a tingle to his spine and set his mind racing in speculative thought.

With a faraway look in his eyes, he could sit on a dusty bench and hear voices from the past. He could see and hear a young couple as they enjoyed the house after it was first built. Then there would be the gurgle of a baby's voice, the patter of small feet on the bedroom floor upstairs. The child would grow up and there would be the sad good-by as he left home. The explorer would hear the shuffling of aged feet, and then—silence. "The roof begins to leak, the floor sags, the windows are broken, the chimney begins to crumble, and now—just an abandoned house with memories," he once penned after exploring a tumbledown dwelling. And then the application: "The old crumbling shack is not the end of the story—the occupants live on—somewhere; but the question echos—*where?* Yes, the dust shall return to the earth—the hut decays—but the *spirit*, where has it gone? . . . Build your home where decay never comes and moth and rust do not corrupt!"

When Class members met or observed Dr. DeHaan for the first time, many were surprised—and many had mental pictures shattered. That he wore no halo and could appear and be so human encouraged some and ruffled others. At Bible conference centers, early risers were likely to meet him dressed casually, fishing rod and tackle box in hand, heading for a nearby lake. His ability always to be himself, however, had a great effect on most.

While the influence of his preaching reached far and wide, in his daily life M. R. DeHaan was no different than other men. He had to work at being a good father and husband. And he spent some of his happiest hours of life dressed in old clothes, shoveling manure from his barn and working among the vegetables in his well-tended garden.

CHAPTER 11

THE FARMER OF
LEONARD STREET

"Abide in me, and I in you. As the branch cannot bear fruit of itself, except it
abide in the vine, no more can ye, except ye abide in me."
JOHN 15:4

Those who listened closely over the years to M. R. DeHaan
and read his writings, especially his meditations in *Our
Daily Bread*, sensed it: he was a farmer at heart. Shortly after he
assumed the pastorate of Calvary Undenominational Church,
he moved his family into a two-story white frame house at
2515 Leonard Street on the edge of northwest Grand Rapids.
It was springtime when the DeHaans moved, and brightly col-
ored daffodils, tulips, and crocuses greeted them. Young elms
spoke of comfortable, restful days ahead for those who would
enjoy their shade, but out back of the house eleven rolling acres
of land challenged the Doctor's green thumb and his outdoor
spirit. Here, when he could be home, he relished putting on
old clothes and a battered hat to do chores about the barn or to
cultivate his vegetable garden. And it was here that he enjoyed
the lively years as the four DeHaan children grew up.

When the DeHaans moved to Leonard Street, Marvin was five and looking forward to first grade. Ruth was fifteen and in high school, June was twelve and anxious for the day when she would be in school with Ruth, and Richard was a mischievous eight.

With Dad often away from home, Priscilla had the task of maintaining discipline. But if he was around, he didn't hesitate to use his belt to punish misbehavior. According to June, her father was a man who meant what he said. "His whole personality was that way—he always did what he said he was going to do," she said.

Strong father figure that he was, Dr. DeHaan stood for no foolishness among his offspring. Take meals, for example. Despite pangs of hunger, the children were expected to sit reverently through a rather lengthy blessing uttered fervently by their father. After dinner, with appetites satisfied and the young children anxious to return to their activities, the family obediently sat through a devotional time. This usually consisted of Dad's reading Scripture and praying, though other family members also sometimes participated. Generally, as the children grew older, they appreciated these times together; but if anyone didn't, he or she dared not show it when Dad was in charge.

Things were more informal when Dad was away, and occasionally at devotional time matters got a bit out of hand. Perhaps young Marv would begin to giggle, and then June would catch it, until everyone had the giggles, including Priscilla.

The fact that their father was a physician as well as a minister made the DeHaan children think of him as an extra-special person. He never over-doctored them, however, treating the usual illnesses quite casually, sometimes to the distress of his wife. He prescribed aspirin for colds and other minor

ailments, taking the attitude that these illnesses had to run
their courses.

Dad also set several broken bones when the children suffered growing-up spills. When June broke an arm while roller-
skating, Priscilla called him and he was there within minutes.
Taking a careful, compassionate look, he said, "I'll give you
fifty cents if you don't cry while I set it." His touch was gentle,
and moments later the ordeal was over, and June was a half
dollar richer and proud possessor of an arm cast. Once when
the family was staying at the Gull Lake Bible Conference where
M.R. was a speaker, Marvin turned up with a broken arm just
before his father was to speak. Working quickly, M.R. calmly
set the arm. Minutes later he was preaching, seeking to minister to conferees with broken lives and spirits.

His love and compassion toward other people made a lasting
impression on his own children. June remembered especially
the family with the mother who was mentally and physically
deficient, unable properly to care for her nine children. "Dad
felt very strongly for these children," June recalled. "Every autumn he outfitted them in shoes and rubbers and other things
they needed."

The children also observed their father's willingness to talk
to people day or night about spiritual and personal problems.
Once the children were hustled out of the room when a couple
came to the DeHaan home seeking help. They learned later that
the man had a revolver and was threatening his wife's life. The
Doctor, through wise counsel, managed to convince them that
God could heal their differences if they would trust Him. They
did so, and the husband gave Dr. DeHaan the revolver.

Holiday times were special for various reasons. Dad set the
tone for Thanksgiving, perhaps the most festive occasion of the
year in the DeHaan home, with a big turkey and all the savory

trimmings. It was a time of merriment and giving thanks to God, led by M.R. at the head of the table. Christmas was a warm, happy time, too, although Dad had deep convictions concerning what he felt was the commemoration of "a day instead of the Man, Christ Jesus." He and Priscilla agreed on a modest, Santa Claus-less observance, as he faced the fact that Christmas was "here to stay—till Jesus comes to put an end to Christmas," as he put it.

Without doubt the warm heart their father had toward the Word of God made a tremendous impact on the four DeHaan children. Richard trusted Christ when he was about ten years of age. "We had a good Sunday school teacher and I was really convicted one Sunday morning," he recalled. "I went home, got down on my knees, and accepted Christ as my Savior. But I know the preaching I heard Sunday after Sunday from Dad had made its impact upon me." Richard's conversion had some influence on Marv, who when he was about seven came to Christ following a Sunday service conducted by his father at Calvary Undenominational Church. June trusted Christ when she was eight in a Sunday evening service at Calvary Reformed Church, and Ruth committed her life to the Savior under her father's ministry when she was eleven, also at Calvary Reformed Church.

In addition to communicating well with his children in regard to spiritual matters, the Doctor was a master in other areas also. Ruth, for example, told of times when he would take her out on nature walks and point out various spring flowers, calling them all by name. There were times when he would excitedly get everyone out of bed to show them the northern lights or to watch a storm. That's the big reason Ruth said she never feared storms. "He would sometimes take us out on the back porch during a severe electrical storm and exclaim, 'Isn't this beautiful! My Father is making it all!'"

He enjoyed taking the family on rides over the worst back roads and the most rickety bridges he could find, pointing out wonders of nature as they bounced along. Because of his vast knowledge of a myriad of subjects, he stimulated the children to broaden their minds. Conversations on these back-road trips, and at home, were extremely lively, sometimes to the point of sounding like a family quarrel as they exchanged information and ideas.

※　※　※

Living as they did on their father's little farm, the DeHaan children not only benefited from the fresh vegetables, fruit, milk, eggs, honey, and other products, but their minds became repositories for bits of information on the best methods of operating a farm. They learned firsthand the need for pruning grapevines and for removing the suckers from below the graft on pear trees. They learned that asparagus loves salt and thrives on it, but that salt is death to weeds, as they watched Dad spread generous amounts of salt evenly over the asparagus plot in early spring.

Marv and Richard learned a memorable lesson—and a painful one for Richard—the day they accompanied Dad in the field among his beehives. One of the bees zeroed in on Richard and, before he knew it, stung him just above the eye. He hit at it and threw himself in the grass, kicking and screaming. No sooner had the bee been brushed away than it went straight for Marv and began buzzing around his head while he, too, hid his head in the grass, screaming and calling for help.

Dad, the beekeeper, thoroughly schooled in the habits of bees from considerable reading and observation, picked Marv up and told him to stop crying. "The bee is harmless. It cannot hurt you. It has lost its sting," he said. He took him over to his elder brother, showed him the little black stinger in his brother's brow, and then said, "When the bee leaves its stinger in the victim, from then on it is perfectly harmless. The bee can still buzz and scare you, but it is powerless to hurt you. Your brother took the sting away by being stung." Then, unable to resist a sermon, he explained 1 Corinthians 15:55: "'O death, where is thy sting? O grave, where is thy victory?' The Lord Jesus, 'our elder Brother,' hung on the cross and took the sting out of death, namely sin; and now death, which has only one sting, can no longer hurt us," he explained in some detail.

The Doctor was a lover of animals, and this interest added considerably to the good times the family had together. Mike, a bulldog, was his constant companion at home for sixteen years. Mike—short for Microbe "because he was so small" when he was given to the family—cleared the farm of woodchucks and rats. At one stage the family had a pet sheep and a raccoon that would get peanuts out of the Doctor's pockets. But the most memorable pets were the crows Dad brought in on separate occasions. He got one of the miserable pets from a nest in the woods and for a time kept it in a box beside the kitchen stove until it grew feathers. After learning to fly, it would steal clothespins from the line and send garments fluttering to the ground. When June went out to pick strawberries, the mischievous crow chased her into the house on more than one occasion. Another of Dad's crows stole a neighbor's pork chops from her kitchen table, threatening the warm friendship that existed between the two families.

❈   ❈   ❈

As the children grew, their father often showed unusual understanding of their youthful problems. When they were old enough to drive, for example, he was generous with the family car, letting the boys use it on dates. And when Marv wrecked the car, his father had no harsh words for him, nor on the two or three other occasions when he came home with dented fenders. June got two speeding tickets within a few weeks of each other. As strict a disciplinarian as he was, her father realized that she was completely shaken by the experience and he offered no stinging reprimand. "I always think of the verse in James, 'The Lord upbraideth not,'" said June. "Dad was that way. He never rubbed it in afterward."

But M.R. was not as understanding when Marv went away to college and in his senior year insisted on buying an "old klunker" from his cousin. A college boy had no business with a car, he told Marv in clear terms. Later, when Marv fell in love with Marilyn Johnson while he was in Chicago Medical School, Dr. DeHaan had some strong father-to-son advice. "Take it easy," he urged. "Before you marry, wait until you're through med school and ready to go into practice." *Like I did*, he could have added. But boys will be boys, and Marv married his last year in med school, with his father officiating.

It was a source of great satisfaction to the Doctor that he not only delivered all four of his children at birth but that he also tied the matrimonial knots for them. Even though he wanted his sons and daughters to marry Christians, which each did, he never tried to choose mates for any of them. He put at least one to the test, however, to determine how strong he was in the faith.

When Ruth invited Tony Haaksma for dinner for the first time at the DeHaan home, her father asked the young man to say the blessing at the table. Tony had trusted Christ when he was seventeen under Dr. DeHaan's ministry, but it was with much difficulty that he prayed in the presence of the Doctor. Despite this embarrassing beginning, after his marriage to Ruth, Tony and his father-in-law became warm companions, talking easily with one another and fishing together often. Much the same relationship existed between the Doctor and June's husband, Rich Boone.

M. R. DeHaan was proud of his family. It warmed his heart that Marvin chose to go into medicine, although it distressed him that, following an arm injury in the mid-1960s, Marvin had to quit surgery. He returned to school and later became a practicing psychiatrist. It also pleased him that both Ruth and June became nurses and that Richard's wife, Marge, was a nurse.

Later, when grandchildren began to arrive, M.R. bounced them on his knee until they were old enough to accompany him on trips to the barn and help him pick beans, tomatoes, strawberries, corn, and other bounty from his garden. In all, he and Priscilla ultimately had twelve grandsons—"The Twelve Apostles," he called them. Then on September 5, 1960, the Marvin DeHaans added the thirteenth grandchild, a girl.

As much as he loved his grandchildren, however, the Doctor was not a doting grandfather. Despite the fact that he often had a movie camera aimed at them, if he felt they weren't being disciplined properly, he said so. He never showered them with gifts but rather with knowledge of God and His marvelous world. Of course, those grandchildren who profited most were those who lived nearby. Marvin and his wife, Marilyn, and their family lived in Wheaton, Illinois; June and her husband,

Richard Boone, and family lived in Waukeshaw, Wisconsin. But Richard and his family, as well as Ruth and her family, lived in homes built on their father's Leonard Street property.

Ruth's son David, the eldest grandchild, who later worked for Radio Bible Class in its book department, took over the DeHaan garden when his grandfather's health began to fail. He always remembered his grandfather's calm reaction when his palomino mare was giving birth to a colt. David burst into the DeHaan kitchen, shouting the news. "I have to call the veterinarian! Penny is having a baby!" M.R. quieted David with the assurance it was quite a natural process; and with a little assistance from Grandfather, Penny gave birth to a splendid mare colt. David watched with delight as thirty minutes later she struggled to her feet and "went straight to the cafeteria," as his grandfather once described it, "and soon was gurgling and nursing to her heart's content."

Even the grandchildren who did not live in Grand Rapids saw their grandfather often enough to have him make an impact on them. June's sons, Jon and Rick Boone, for example, recalled that when fishing with Grandpa, Jon would row the boat and at the same time learn lessons from him concerning the habits of fish. Rick enjoyed the automobile rides and other activities during which his grandfather would teach him to recognize the different trees and various animals. By his mid-teens, Rick had become such an animal lover that he had a home zoo, including rats, turtles, and snakes.

Richard's oldest son, Mart, says that some of his earliest memories of his grandfather were of his grandfather on his knees. Mart and his three brothers grew up in a house on the back of their grandparents' property, and Mart remembers his grandfather on his knees weeding the family garden, shooting crows in the pine trees, or cleaning fish caught in one of the many West Michigan lakes.

＊　＊　＊

M. R. DeHaan liked nothing better than to drink deeply from the world that his heavenly Father had so magnificently fashioned. Even while he worked in his study at home, sights and sounds of nature interrupted him and put him in a trance at his window: a robin on her nest calmly riding out a fierce storm . . . a wise little chipmunk scampering about on a bright fall day storing food for the winter months ahead . . . brash crows taunting a stolid gray owl . . . a choir of birds lustily singing after a spring shower . . . a well-camouflaged tree frog playing hide-and-seek and serenading from a nearby elm. These and a thousand more sights and sounds held the Doctor spellbound and often colorfully enlivened his devotional meditations.

While he enjoyed hunting, until he gave it up for health reasons, the Doctor rated fishing as his number one outdoor interest. Over the years this adventurous sport took him into trout streams in Michigan, Wisconsin, Kentucky, the Colorado Rockies, and Canada, into Puget Sound, waters off the Florida coast, and bass lakes elsewhere. From an outdoor viewpoint, he was never happier than when he had a fly rod in his hand and a fishing buddy at his side—a grandson, a son or son-in-law, or sidekicks such as Frank O'Dell and Jake De Vogel, men of a similar stocky build whose rugged personalities dovetailed perfectly with the Doctor's.

It was in the summer of 1945, however, on a visit to Norway, a town in upper Michigan, to fish with another friend, Dad Asp, and preach in a small church in the area, that M.R. was introduced to a place he came to love more than any other spot in the vast outdoor wonderland—and to two people who were to become part of his inner circle of friends.

Rachel Carlson, whose heart hungered for a firmer grasp of the truths of God's Word, had driven the twelve miles from Iron Mountain to Norway to hear Dr. DeHaan preach. Afterward she greeted him and, mentioning that she had heard of his interest in fishing, half-jestingly invited him to the cottage she and her husband, Clarence, owned on a good fishing lake just over the border from Iron Mountain in Wisconsin. To the Carlsons' surprise, M.R. took them up on the offer, and a few weeks later he and Priscilla traveled to the cottage.

Nestled in a vast virgin forest high above Patton (also spelled Patten) Lake, the cottage, appropriately named "Rest-a-While," captured M.R.'s heart from the beginning. Its primitiveness made him feel like a pioneer: a hard-to-operate water pump out front, a woodstove, gas light in the living room and kerosene lamps in other rooms, a dilapidated dock, and an old-fashioned outhouse painted green. In the mid-1950s the Carlsons modernized "Rest-a-While," putting in electricity, running water, toilet facilities, and additional rooms, including a dining room overlooking the lake, and a new dock. The upstairs was made into three rooms, and one room was set aside especially for the DeHaans. M.R. tried to dissuade Clarence and Rachel from modernizing, but he soon appreciated everything they had done—from the instant heat to the modern kitchen where he brewed coffee before going on the lake for a morning's catch.

In the Carlsons' minds, "Rest-a-While" became M. R. DeHaan's cottage—a place where the man they came to love so deeply could relax and unwind, away from the phone and office. They gave him everything but the deed, as he and Priscilla and various other members of the family visited the cottage spring and fall, year after year. There the Doctor fished, wrote, and feasted on the sights about him. As the sun rose, the lake became a gray-blue mirror, until a breeze began to play upon it, turning it to shimmering diamonds. Crisp autumn mornings unfurled azure skies that accented colorful foliage along the shoreline—exciting crimson and scarlet sumac and red maples, luscious yellow of the birches, quaking aspens, and dark green spruces, hemlocks, and pines. In afternoons, fleecy clouds began a swift, endless parade of changing shapes from the west.

"My Father painted it all!" the entranced Doctor said time and again.

On the lake itself, whether rowing his stubby brown boat or chugging along powered by his three-horse Evinrude, the Doctor drank in the glories of the unspoiled wilderness, fascinated by bald eagles, blue herons, and geese. He was intrigued by the four-footed wildlife—skittish deer, the sly and elusive red fox, and the black bear nibbling blueberries in a clearing—and by the slithering reptiles that wriggled through the forest undergrowth.

In the north woods, particularly on moonless nights, myriads of stars spangled the pitch-black sky. "I have just come in from outdoors and I am dizzy and amazed," M.R. once penned. "With my field glasses, I swept the heavens and came to a new appreciation of the words of David, 'When I consider Thy heavens . . . what is man . . .?'" (Psalm 8:3–4).

Everywhere he looked, the teacher of Radio Bible Class saw Bible truths revealed. "He could look at anything in nature and come up with a story that had to do with redemption," said Clarence Carlson. "Whether it was fish, a tree, or an animal, he could see the handwriting of God and its relationship to the Word of God. Take the lake, for example. He talked about how it sustained life and how it could also take life. It would hold you up, but it could also take your life if you were not in a boat. So, as he pointed out, the Word of God has the power also to take your life or to sustain your life. If you didn't drink water, you would die—and he'd drink water right out of his hat! This was true of God's Word, he said: you had to drink it to live."

As the years passed, M. R. DeHaan and Clarence Carlson—a soft-spoken, perceptive man about ten years DeHaan's junior—became the warmest of friends. They fished together and shared thoughts from the Bible, with Clarence generally on the receiving end. Once the manufacturer of about 80 percent of the wooden handles and backing for rubber stamps used in the United States, Carlson described himself as a rather wobbly Christian until he encountered DeHaan.

"After I got to know the truth of the grace of God, I started to teach Sunday school," Carlson said. "I grew in the knowledge of the Word so that after a while I was able to study by myself. Sometimes I'd come out to the cottage and the Doctor would go over a chapter for me verse by verse, pointing out details and outlines that I could bring out to my Sunday school class. He'd sit for hours and just talk to me. If he wasn't in the area, I'd call him long distance to talk over some point of Scripture. The Doctor gave me a message. He taught me what it means to be justified by faith. And the second coming and the righteousness of God he just opened up in a marvelous way."

Mrs. Carlson shared a similar story: as a result of her contact with Dr. DeHaan, she grew considerably in her spiritual life and became a person capable of teaching others.

When the Carlsons dropped in on the DeHaans on a warm evening, they might find him stripped to the waist and barefoot, resting in the living room with Mrs. DeHaan. After dressing, including white shirt and tie, he would teach the Carlsons from the Bible as if they were a large audience.

Clarence Carlson told of how, because of M. R. DeHaan, he began to rethink his position on eternal security. He frankly told the Doctor that he believed a Christian could "fall from grace" through sinning. "The Doctor took hold of me, marched me behind the cottage, looked me square in the eye and said, 'Clarence, if it isn't *all of grace*, we're all sunk!' It convinced me so much that I started to study, and it wasn't too long before I really had my eyes opened to this marvelous truth of the security of the believer in Christ."

The Carlsons asserted that much of the fundamental Bible teaching in the Iron Mountain area grew out of Dr. DeHaan's visits. At the cottage he conducted Bible studies for friends the Carlsons invited in, and he preached in small local country churches to congregations of thirty or forty on many occasions. He talked to the residents and vacationers at the lake, knowing many personally and sharing the gospel with them.

Once in Iron Mountain the Doctor sat waiting his turn in a crowded barbershop when a loudmouth came in and quipped to a barber, "I've got a good bargain for you. I can get you a ticket straight through to heaven for $25, and when you get there, if you don't like it, you can come back and I'll give you your money back and you can go to hell."

There were a few guffaws, but not from the smoldering Doctor. His gravel voice ground out: "I can get you a ticket straight through to heaven for free. That price was paid by Jesus Christ on Calvary two thousand years ago."

The loudmouth chided, "You don't believe that stuff!"

With his blood pressure rising, Dr. DeHaan cut loose with a tongue-lashing that gave the man a barbershop trimming he hadn't bargained for, and he left, his neck red and hair uncut.

Dr. DeHaan did not hesitate to deal severely with anyone who flippantly handled God's truths. Even for Christians who misquoted Scripture, he had a sharp word of reprimand.

❋   ❋   ❋

Without doubt the most important human element in the life of M. R. DeHaan was his wife, Priscilla. Calm, steady, even-tempered, she was the balance wheel that kept the sometimes high, sometimes low Doctor ticking just right. For him there seemed to be no medium mood as he kept up with the tremendous load of work that he carried. Never a nagger, "Mother," as he usually called her, had just the right word, the right touch, the right look, and knew how to handle delicate situations.

When he was going through rough days at Calvary Reformed Church and later at Calvary Undenominational Church, Priscilla quieted him, encouraged him, and prayed with him. She answered anonymous phone calls, sometimes listening to mean-spirited attacks meant for him. Priscilla wished to protect her husband whenever possible.

In day-to-day household matters, she knew what to cook to please him, although he did not have a finicky appetite. He was mainly a meat-and-vegetable man, occasionally enjoying potatoes with lots of salt, and had a taste for certain spicy dishes. Pea soup was his favorite, and he could make a meal on a large bowlful. He didn't care a lot about desserts, but she knew she could delight him with peaches and cream.

It was Priscilla who helped keep M.R. dressed neatly—except when he was at home in his gardening clothes. Left to his own devices, he might have showed up at Radio Bible Class with rumpled trousers and scuffed shoes, but Priscilla pressed his trousers and kept his shoes polished. Besides all this, she patiently sat by as he carried on his work in his study into the night hours.

Although M.R. was a man who enjoyed talking with people, he usually tagged along reluctantly with Priscilla to social gatherings. But he did enjoy getting together with one group, made up of several couples from their Calvary Undenominational Church days, who for many years gathered for anniversaries and other occasions. In most social situations, M.R. tended to dominate conversations, usually turning discussions to matters relating to Scripture. In a sense, the party would end up as a two-hour Bible lesson, probably on world conditions and prophecy. If this didn't happen and the conversation degenerated to chitchat, the Doctor preferred to drop into a comfortable chair and sleep. But even in these instances, Priscilla showed understanding, calmly accepting it as part of the makeup of the man she married.

M.R. occasionally enjoyed referring to Priscilla in sermon illustrations. He claimed he never really understood his wife. "This vase must stand exactly here, and that figurine must be there—not an inch either way," he once wrote. "The salad must sleep on a bed of rabbit food—lettuce, water cress, or some other cattle feed. The meat must be decorated with parsley. The cherry on the dessert must rest right on top of the pudding. Yes, women are different, and how glad I am. What a drab world it would be if they had no more sense of beauty, adornment, and artistic arrangement than we men. And so while we don't understand them, we *appreciate* them."

Once he humorously claimed he had been married to six different wives and was then living with his seventh. Quickly, he explained that "science tells us that we get a new body every seven years. The cells of our bodies are used up in the process of metabolism, and there is a complete change of tissue every seven years. But the soul and spirit remain the same. Though the house changes, the occupant remains the same. Therefore, in our forty-four years of married life, I've had six wives—but in reality the same wife, a *wonderful* one!"

Being the man of high-low temperament that he was, M.R. did not always treat Priscilla like the queen he really considered her to be. On one occasion the Holy Spirit convicted him through a meditation he himself had written. Arriving at the office one morning, he told the story:

"This morning Mrs. DeHaan and I had a little disagreement, and I didn't say anything at all as we ate breakfast. Finally it was time to read the devotional in *Our Daily Bread*. She did so silently to herself for a moment. Then taking it and shoving it under my nose, she asked, 'Are you the man who wrote this?' I read the article and felt about an inch tall. It had to do with kindness and forbearance. That did it. We had to make up right there. It's so easy to preach but so much more difficult to practice."

M. R. DeHaan was a man of God and a great Bible teacher, but he was also human, and that meant he could sometimes be difficult. Through the years, when God convicted him about such matters, he listened and sometimes was able to reconcile with those with whom he had become estranged in the past. Some of those were men who had been his strongest supporters at Calvary Undenominational Church but had become disenchanted with him toward the end of his ministry there. This was also true of some of the men from his days in the Reformed Church.

One of these men described his meeting with Dr. DeHaan years later as a time of wonderful fellowship. Unforgettable for him were the Doctor's words reflecting on his ministries at Calvary Reformed and Calvary Undenominational. "Young man," he said, "learn a lesson from me. I did everything in haste and in anger." Still another Reformed Church minister reported that after talking with Dr. DeHaan in later years and asking him "If you had to do it all over again, and this would mean dividing a church, would you do it?" the Doctor replied, "No."[1]

There was one estrangement, however, that shook M. R. DeHaan to the core—one that he hadn't foreseen, one that he himself could not resolve.

---

1. Boslooper, *Grace and Glory Days*, 99.

HEARTBREAK

"Unto thee will I cry, O LORD my rock; be not silent to me . . . ."
PSALM 28:1

R ichard DeHaan had worked with the *Radio Bible Class* broadcast in one way or another since he was fifteen years old, and it was no secret that he was considered his father's successor in the ministry. Needless to say, then, the Doctor was jolted when Richard told him he didn't believe he was the person to succeed him.

In the late 1950s, Richard, now himself a man of vision and maturity, began to see the possibilities of expanding the ministry into the growing medium of television. Richard loved his father and had deep respect for his ability to preach and teach the Word, and he believed that this was a way of expanding his father's teaching and reaching a new generation. He envisioned relocating Radio Bible Class to St. Petersburg, Florida, and building a Bible conference that would be used to televise his father's teaching. With a large auditorium, the ministry also could offer Bible conferences with various Bible teachers and an opportunity for vacationing or retired Class members to visit the headquarters and be a part of the broadcast. As a bonus, living costs would be less, and the warmer climate would be beneficial to employees. There would be no snow to shovel and no biting zero days—a factor to consider for his aging father with his heart condition.

Richard and John Camp, head of the J. M. Camp and Company advertising agency, which represented Radio Bible Class to radio stations, visited St. Petersburg on several occasions and found suitable property. The Doctor went down to look over the situation, and the men talked of the advantage of Florida as they played shuffleboard. M.R. looked at the property but decided against it when he discovered another tract that he liked better. Radio Bible Class purchased the land, M.R. knelt on the property and prayed a prayer of dedication, and Richard began mentally mapping out plans for relocation.

That did not settle the matter, however, for M.R. continued to vacillate on the matter of television and the Florida location, uncertain that this was the right move. Finally, he told Richard he had changed his mind. God had blessed Radio Bible Class in Grand Rapids, and the people there had been good to the Class. This was home. The move to television was out, and the headquarters would remain in Grand Rapids.

Richard was deeply disappointed. He and others had worked hard on the project, and he was convinced that television was an important part of the future of the ministry. Along with this was the fact that staff members who were moving to Florida had put their homes on the market, and at least one family had sold their home. Frustration erupted into anger, which widened the gap between father and son, and Richard decided to leave Radio Bible Class. Thus, in April 1963 he and Marge packed up their belongings and their four children—Mart, Rick, Kurt, and Steve—and headed for St. Petersburg, Florida, without knowing what he would do.

For a long time, in an increasing way, Richard had felt uncomfortable living in the shadow of a great man. He felt that people were accepting him primarily because he was the son of M. R. DeHaan. Did he himself really have something to offer? Occasionally he would fill a speaking engagement for his father, and when he did, he knew some people were comparing him with his father. The thought would occur over and over: *They wanted Dad, not me.* Unable to discuss these matters with his father, he suffered silently, asking God to reveal His will, to make it clear where he should serve. Perhaps this was the opportunity to find that place.

❋   ❋   ❋

When Richard left, M.R. was devastated. For him, the future of Radio Bible Class was wrapped up in his eldest son. Business went on as usual at the office, but his heart was heavy. Richard's name, which was listed as associate teacher, disappeared from the monthly newsletter without explanation. At various times guest speakers taught on the broadcast—Dr. Paul Van Gorder, Dr. Charles Woodbridge, Jack Wyrtzen, and Dr. Richard Seume. Some listeners wrote to ask why.

"We want to be ready in a case of emergency to have some of God's chosen men available to carry on without interruption of the program," was Dr. DeHaan's response. "God has been so gracious, so that in the many years of broadcasting we have missed very few Sundays. However, we realize that sickness, accident, or some other hindrance might make it impossible [for me] to take care of a particular broadcast. We must then be ready to call on one of God's men to fill in."

For Richard, those days were equally painful. He knew that
his father was deeply hurt. But so was he. Later, he spoke of that
time in these words:

> I cherish the associations and influence of being brought up
> in the shadow of a great man such as Dad. But there are
> some psychological disadvantages. I knew people were com-
> paring me to Dad. I had some pretty serious doubts then
> as to whether or not I had what it would take to fill Dad's
> shoes. Being tied down with so many administrative activi-
> ties, I just could not give myself to studying the Word the
> way I felt I had to if I were to take over. My feeling was that
> I should get away from [Grand Rapids] and away from the
> work and just concentrate fully on study and going out into
> a Bible-teaching ministry.
>
> My leaving was one of the toughest things I ever had to do.
> I had the deepest respect and love for Dad, and the fact that
> he misunderstood my motives made leaving all the worse. I
> don't say I didn't do anything wrong. But I have great confi-
> dence in the sovereignty of God and that He overrules in the
> affairs of His children. I know that my breaking away and
> going to St. Petersburg was the best thing that could have
> happened to me.

Those were also difficult times financially for Richard and
his family. For a while he filled pulpits, and he got his real es-
tate license. Then he was asked to help a local youth ministry in
the St. Petersburg area in their radio ministry to young people,
and for a year Richard conducted a radio program for teenagers. Richard maintained contact with his parents primarily
through his mother, who then read his letters to M.R.

In Grand Rapids, Dr. DeHaan carried on his ministry with the same fervency as always, but he was saddened by Richard's absence and the estrangement between them. He was also facing the reality of his age and his health. He could not go on forever. Who would ultimately take over the worldwide ministry?

While M.R. still wanted his son back with the broadcast, he wouldn't beg or cajole. If God wanted Richard back on the broadcast and prepared to take over in the future, He would work out the details. That was one side of the Doctor's thinking. On the other side, he felt hurt and saddened that the months were passing without any signs of their being reunited in the ministry. He confided in a number of friends and associates, and his son Marvin, seeking encouragement and wondering what he had done wrong.

Meanwhile, as the months passed, Richard saw God close door after door. Attractive offers came—and then evaporated for one reason or another. The pastor of a large church commented in the hearing of one of Richard's friends: "When I retire, Richard DeHaan is the only person who could fill the bill here." Such experiences and comments, however, served to build the confidence of a man who wondered sometimes if all he had was his father's coattail.

Richard spent hours in the Word daily and alone with God, seeking to know Him more intimately. He searched his heart as he read and studied the Scriptures, and the Word of God became more alive than ever to him. A gentle peace began to flood his heart.

Some months after he left Grand Rapids, Richard returned for a visit with his father. The two discussed the possibility of his return, but the time proved unfruitful and Richard returned to Florida. He was convinced that if he were ever to return to the broadcast in Grand Rapids, he would need clear signals from God, and by late 1964 he still had no leading in that direction.

CHAPTER 13

PERHAPS TODAY

"There is laid up . . . a crown of righteousness . . . unto all them also that love his appearing."
2 TIMOTHY 4:8

From his chair at one end of the long birch table in the sun-parlor-like, knotty pine dining room in "Rest-a-While" cottage, M. R. DeHaan scrawled countless manuscript pages of meditations and books. As he gazed through the picture window at the sparkling waters of Patton Lake, the constantly changing scene quickened his pulse and pen. He also gained inspiration enough in other spots in the area to turn out reams of manuscript copy on his busman's holidays in northern Wisconsin. Once he sat on a logging bridge and penned a meditation as the singing, dancing river inspired these thoughts:

> There are three stanzas to my song. The first is about my source, the second is about my journey, and the third is about my goal.
>
> The source is a never-failing spring deep in the hills. Isaiah tells us that "the glorious Lord will be to us a place of broad rivers and streams" (Isaiah 33:21). The peace of God's

river is not monotony but constant variety; there are rapids, runs, waterfalls, and peaceful pools. So, too, the heart at peace with God experiences all the vicissitudes of life, of weal and woe, of joy and sorrow—but—at the same time— always *peace*. The goal of the river is the ocean—even so we too must lose ourselves in the ocean of God's love, for only then will our peace know its fullness in the eternal rest. Can you imagine! I used to think a river was good only for catching fish!

Dr. DeHaan used 8½" x 11" typing paper, writing in ink with a strong, steady hand, and unconcerned with margins. His style was relatively simple and down to earth, flowing smoothly, his thoughts easy to follow. Usually he was up early writing, a couple of hours ahead of his wife, or other members of the family who might be staying with them. Later, back at the office, he presented his handwritten manuscript to his secretary, Lee (as he called Leona Hertel), trusting her to make minor corrections as she typed it.

When in Grand Rapids, the Doctor did much of his writing in his study at home. He used few reference books, usually the only volume open on his desk being a well-marked King James Bible. (He abhorred most of the new versions, branding them "versions and perversions.") Like other writers, he hit dry periods, and stared out the window hoping for a sudden inspiration. Once he sat there "thinking, thinking, without a worthwhile idea entering my head," he later wrote.

I was trying desperately to get an inspiration for an article for *Our Daily Bread* but nothing would come. Disappointedly, I gave up, walked outside, and stretched myself on the grass— and *looked up*. And there was my inspiration. I slipped into one of those pleasant moods of reverie, where imagination runs free and easy. I imagined those fleecy clouds were living things traversing the skies to meet for some joyous occasion. There was a fleecy cloud shaped exactly like a gamboling lamb. And there was a huge gray elephant with trunk and all. Another cloud became a giant ship loaded with people, while over in the west there were islands of sun-drenched beauty. Faces began to appear, faces of loved ones—and then two clouds folded together, and, as the sun streaked their edges with a snow-white border of light, the face of all faces, beautiful beyond description, was formed in fleeting outline, and then the vapors tumbled apart. But I had seen a face—unlike any other. With eyes fixed upon the rift in the clouds, peering into the endless depth of blue, I visualized that day when He shall come and we shall "*see His face.*"

Dr. DeHaan went on to say that he awakened from his reverie and realized it was "not all a dream, for *He is coming again—it could be today!*"

If any doctrine excited M. R. DeHaan above another, it was the doctrine of the second coming of Jesus Christ. From his early days as a preacher and teacher, he had proclaimed the glad news of the coming again of the God-Man. One man, after hearing the Doctor preach at Moody Bible Institute's Founders Week conference, said he had heard many preachers speak about the return of the Lord. "But," he said, "they spoke about it like they were delivering a lecture. Dr. DeHaan moved me tremendously because here was a man who really *believed* the Lord was coming back as a practical reality." DeHaan devoted many pages to the subject in his twenty-five books and numerous booklets, and wrote about it in countless devotional articles. His books giving major emphasis to the return of Christ are *The Second Coming of Jesus* (1944), *Signs of the Times* (1951), and *Coming Events in Prophecy* (1962).

In *Coming Events in Prophecy* he wrote:

> As we look upon conditions in the world today, if we did not have this hope of Christ's returning, and we had to rely upon the power of the Church, and the testimony of Christians to bring about the cessation of hostilities and to bring in perfect righteousness, I for one would despair and give up hope entirely. If I did not believe in the imminent, personal return of the Lord Jesus to make right that which is all wrong in this world today, and to bring in the peace for which man has so long been sighing, and for which he has so long been looking, I don't think I would care to preach another sermon. I would have to admit that the whole thing is a failure, and that the Gospel has not accomplished that which we had expected it to do, and that Christianity is nothing else but another religion and a tremendous farce.

But pointing out that Christ's last promise to His disciples was that He was coming again and that the last promise of the Bible is "surely I come quickly" (Revelation 20:20), he wrote, "Just as surely as Jesus came and died on the cross the first time, and arose from the grave, and ascended into heaven, He is coming again; coming again to put a stop to all the wickedness and all the inequality and iniquity of this present day, put an end to man's rule of failure and bungling, and to set up His glorious Millennial Kingdom."

Hardly a day passed without the Doctor making some reference to the imminent return of the Lord. He talked about it with co-workers and others, and he often spoke of it in the regular devotional times for the staff at Radio Bible Class. The thought did more to give him a good start for each day than his early morning coffee.

An Australian listener to the *Radio Bible Class* broadcast sent Dr. DeHaan an attractive plaque proclaiming, "Perhaps Today." He put it on the edge of his desk facing the door. It was the first thing he looked at as he entered his office. "It reminds me of the tremendous responsibility of this one day [I am living now], because the motto is certainly true according to the promise of the Book, *perhaps today*," he wrote in 1964.

At the beginning of every year, he said, "I am looking for the Lord Jesus to come this year. But if He doesn't, then I'll look for Him next year."

In no sense, however, did M.R.'s intense interest in the second coming cause him to lay aside responsibilities and go to a hilltop to await Christ's return. While the Doctor believed the Lord might come at any moment, he kept busy, "instant in season, out of season" (2 Timothy 4:2), faithfully, fervently getting out the gospel to far-flung areas.

Whatever M. R. DeHaan believed, he believed thoroughly. Once an associate asked him how he "leaned" on a certain theological question. Characteristically, he retorted: "I never like lean-to's. I'm either in one tent or another. I'm never in a lean-to." He smiled. "If I know it, I know it; if I don't, I don't."

In his last book, *Portraits of Christ in Genesis* (published in 1966 after his death), Dr. DeHaan clearly stated his position:

> So often we become disturbed by conditions in the world, the increase in crime, violence, and wickedness, the rapid spread of Communism, the apostasy of the Church, and the threat of a great racial struggle or an atomic conflict. . . . But all these things have been foretold and are under the

complete control of our God. . . . As a preacher of the Gospel, I have that one commission, "Preach the Word" (2 Timothy 4:2), and when I depart from this to join the forces which would bring in a man-made Great Society, I am unfaithful to my calling. It is not my business as a preacher to spend my time in civil rights demonstrations, or seeking to bring a Utopia on earth during this dispensation. My one task shall be to preach the Word, not expecting to solve the problems of the nations until Jesus comes.

WELCOME HOME

*"In my Father's house are many mansions: if it were not so, I would have
told you. I go to prepare a place for you."*

JOHN 14:2

When the 10:00 a.m. coffee break bell rang in the offices
of Radio Bible Class on June 25, 1964, eighty employees
laid aside their work and went downstairs to the lunchroom.
Word had been circulated that everyone was expected for a
special event. When all had gathered, Dr. and Mrs. DeHaan
were asked to come down, the "committee" having arranged
for Priscilla to be in the building that morning. When the
DeHaans entered the lunchroom, a pianist played a few measures of the bridal march to set the atmosphere for this celebra-
tion of the DeHaans' Golden Wedding anniversary.

Among those planning the Golden Wedding coffee break,
however, there were gnawing thoughts that this might be the
last time they could honor Dr. DeHaan in a special manner.
At seventy-three, he showed increased outward signs of failing health, although his mind was still sharp and he often exhibited the bursts of energy for which he was known. Usually
the first to arrive at the office, he had never limited himself to

a forty-hour week, and he didn't now. He continued to tape broadcasts, and there was always writing to do, along with administrative details and speaking engagements. But in an *Our Daily Bread* article in the early 1960s, he himself wrote:

"The Owner of the 'house' I have occupied here on earth has served notice that I must soon move out. He will not make many more repairs—since I am going to vacate it anyway. The foundation is crumbling, the roof leaks, the heating system is failing, and the windows are getting dim. The steps are getting shaky and the hinges are getting rusty and squeaky." Yet, as he added, he didn't dread the thought of "moving": "I have been overwhelmed by the innumerable advantages of that new Home over this old one; so much so that now instead of dreading it, I am beginning to get anxious to move. If it were not for a few things I still have to do, I would want to move pronto."

The Doctor never asked for sympathy. If someone asked how he felt, with a little smile he would answer, "You shouldn't ask me that."

During his declining years, aware of his history of coronaries, he relied to some degree on medication to keep himself going. Once his doctor gave him a prescription, but Dr. DeHaan had already prescribed it for himself and had been "taking twice that much of the same medicine for two years," he confided to an associate.

Because of a tendency to be overweight, the Doctor tried to be moderate in his eating habits. Sometimes invitations out to dinner nullified his good intentions. "Henry, I sinned again," he once told Henry Bosch. "I ate more than I should have. But it was so delicious and they kept pushing it on me."

He continued to take his coffee hot—steaming hot—and extra strong. A cup or two helped him start the day—not as early as in his younger years, but usually not later than 6:30.

Before the coffee, he now talked with the Lord as he lay in bed. "I have learned the value of staying in bed a little while after I awaken," he said, "just to think—pray—and plan my day, all with eternity in view. A few minutes 'seeking first' the things of God . . . in the morning, is time well spent!"

Undoubtedly his close communion with God kept M.R. from becoming a sour, cantankerous person in his last years. Some who had locked horns with him in conferences and knew him as a man of spirit and conviction felt he mellowed as he reached his threescore and ten years. But tell him that and he'd snort, "Don't say that! I know fruit. The next thing after mellow is rotten!" With that his face would break into his half smile.

He was painfully aware of the earthen qualities of the vessel God was using. Though he believed that the atoning work of Christ made him secure in the family of God, he once lamented to a friend that he was bothered by "all the things that I'll have to account for at the judgment seat of Christ." With tears on his cheeks, he acknowledged, however, that he had come a long way: "I was born with a quick temper, and it has taken the grace of God to cool me down."

In February 1965, Dr. DeHaan spoke at the Moody Bible Institute Founders Week conference in Chicago. He puffed his way in below-zero weather to and from Moody Church. The bitter cold, together with his climb up the stairs to his second floor room in a nearby motel, aggravated his heart condition. Though he finished his assignment in traditional style, severe chest pains made it an exhausting experience.

The Founders Week conference proved to be his last public meeting. Upon returning to Grand Rapids, he was hospitalized by his doctor for two weeks. This enforced period of rest gave him new vigor when he resumed his duties. But soon afterward an attack of shingles hit him. He insisted on going to the office,

and his secretary, Leona, scolded, "Don't you know you're sup-
posed to be in bed resting when you have shingles?"

He peered at her from the top of his glasses, a twinkle in
his eyes. "And which medical school did you get your degree
from?" He continued working.

❈   ❈   ❈

In late 1964, M.R. prayed in a way he hadn't dared to pray
before. Kneeling alongside Priscilla in a devotional time one
morning, he poured out his heart to God. He must have felt
much like Abraham as the patriarch lifted the knife, prepared
to slay his son as a sacrifice to God. *"Lord, Richard is Yours. Do
anything with him that You want. I'm willing to lose Richard if
necessary. I want only Your will . . . ."*

God took sixty years to prepare Abraham for his climac-
tic event in the school of faith, and it had taken forty-three in
M.R.'s life of faith since he gave up his medical bag to be a messenger of God. "The Lord never puts us to the test until we
are ready for it," he himself had written in his book *Adventures
in Faith.* "He never sends a trial or test, except He has made
preparation for us to come through victorious. . . . If God had
asked Abraham to sacrifice his son before his time, he would
not have been ready for it. . . . God saw beforehand the purpose
in Abraham's life for which He had called him, and moved on
to that end with unerring persistence. The purpose was finally
to conform Abraham unto the image of God. Everything that
happened had some bearing . . . on this final victory."

Just as God moved in the life of Abraham, He was also working out the details in the life of the aging Bible teacher. A few
days after he turned Richard over to God, his heart was heavy
as he closed the door to his study at home. He felt compelled

to write a letter to his son, but he told no one about it, not even Priscilla. It was his first and only letter to Richard, man to man. He had always left the family correspondence to Priscilla.

A few days later, the mailbox clanged at the home of Richard DeHaan in St. Petersburg, Florida. He immediately recognized the handwriting on the envelope and opened it quickly. Tears burned his eyes as he read the four-page letter written in a familiar large scrawl.

Sunday, January 3, 1965
My dear son Richard:

I have not written you before although I have been tempted to do so many times. I have refrained from doing so for two reasons (1) because I was afraid I might say the wrong thing and (2) because I feared I might be misunderstood. But since your letter of Dec. 27 I feel I must write and frankly tell you what is on my heart. In a couple of months I will (D.V.) be 74 years old and I am fully aware that my physical powers are waning. I cannot ignore the almost daily reminders of this fact. In view of this fact of the inevitable, I have been much exercised in seeking God's will in regard to the future of the Radio Bible Class. With this in mind I have been trying out a number of guest speakers, with the hope of finding one who could share some of the responsibilities of the work and ultimately taking over. . . . In the foreseeable future we will have to choose someone to share the work, or even to take over. If the Lord does not come we will have to face this inevitable move. Time is running out for me and I would be remiss in my responsibility if I ignored this fact.

Before we make any further plans I felt led, after much prayer, to write you this letter to make one more earnest request to try and resolve the rift which has arisen between you and me and your relation to the class. My deepest desire of my heart is still the same, that you might carry on the tradition of the class.

Is there any inclination on your part to come back to the class in whatever capacity the Lord may lead? Richard, you don't know how I have missed you, and the family, and each day I miss you more. I am convinced for the glory of God, the best interest of the class, and your own good that your place is with this work. I have made many mistakes, but I can honestly say I have never knowingly or intentionally said or done anything to injure you. It may seem that way and I am sorry for any such impressions I have given. Please forgive me.

If there is any inclination toward coming back and letting bygones be bygones, I shall make no further plan regarding guest speakers or associates. I shall suspend all further moves till I receive your reaction. I shall give myself to prayer that His will may be done. I am writing this longhand—Mother does not even know I am writing. I want to be influenced only by a pure desire for the glory of God, the advancement of His program, and for your best good. I hope I have made myself clear. Your absence from us, though exceedingly painful, may after all be something which was needed, even though we cannot see it now. I miss you and I need you. May His will be done.

With a father's love for his beloved son,
Dad

To Richard, this letter was a clear answer to months of prayer. As he read and pondered his father's words, he whispered, "All right, Lord, You have shown me. I'm going back."

Before the end of March, the Doctor mentioned to the office staff that he had a special unspoken prayer request, and that afternoon Richard walked into the office. M.R. greeted him warmly, and employees' hearts melted when an announcement was made that Richard had rejoined the staff. The scene that followed was a joyous homecoming.

After he rejoined the Radio Bible Class staff, Richard readily submitted himself to the fact that he had much to learn as the "leader" of the work his dad was turning over to him. He felt that it had been beneficial for him and his father to be apart for a while, for it had allowed both to gain a new perspective of the ministry.

❋   ❋   ❋

A few months later, on the evening of July 29, as M.R. and Priscilla were driving north out of Grand Rapids toward the nearby town of Sparta, the vehicle ahead of them slowed down quickly to make a right turn. M.R. swerved to the left to avoid a collision but then collided head-on with a station wagon on the other side of the highway. M.R. was hospitalized with severe head lacerations, an injured left leg, and extensive damage to his breastbone and ribs. Priscilla was treated and released, having suffered minor injuries. When news of the accident hit the press, calls poured into the Radio Bible Class office from many parts of the United States.

The Doctor was hospitalized for almost two weeks. He bled profusely as a result of the blood-thinning medication he was taking for his heart condition, and his face was black and blue. It was during this period that he heard a broadcast tape that brought tears to his eyes. Recorded earlier for release at that time, he heard Richard making the familiar introduction,

"Now here is my father, Dr. DeHaan." His battered, heavily lined face brightened. "Just thank the Lord, Mother!" he said with great emotion to Priscilla, who sat at his bedside.

When the Doctor was released from the hospital, he was far from well. Since the accident, he had been suffering a recurrence of chest pains. But he soon pushed himself to resume broadcasting and writing, and, against Priscilla's wishes, he continued to drive. One of his first outings was the office picnic on August 27, which had been scheduled for July 30 but postponed because of the accident. Bob Roush phoned from the office to tell the Doctor that someone would pick up the DeHaans and drive them to the event. "No, I'll drive myself," the Doctor snorted. "What do you think I am, an invalid?"

In late summer, M.R. had a hankering to go north once again to "Rest-a-While," but once there, he wasn't strong enough to fish, except while sitting on the lakeside dock. His son-in-law and daughter, Rich and June Boone, drove their parents to the northern Wisconsin cottage, where they enjoyed a few days in the woodland setting the Doctor loved so much. But there were lumps in their throats as the grand old fisherman gathered his fishing gear to take back to Grand Rapids. Before, he had always left it at the cottage.

M.R. now did most of his work at home and seldom visited the office. Recording equipment had been installed in his study so that he could make tapes when he felt strong enough to do so. If he did work at the office, he came home and slept all afternoon, then ate supper and went back to bed exhausted. Yet he had no thought of retiring. He often said, "There's no retirement for the Christian. Don't talk about retirement. The world is too needy; we can't retire!"

As a man of the Book, the Doctor spent endless hours poring over Scriptures. Thoughts of being caught up to be with the Lord quickened his pulse. It was the way he wanted to go. "Perhaps today," he continued to say.

But in early December, seventy-four-year-old DeHaan sensed that God was about to take him by way of the valley. His favorite song had long been, "Where the Gates Swing Outward Never," and he felt he would soon be a resident of that heavenly place. He called three of his grandsons—David, Jim, and Dale Haaksma—who lived nearby, and, like a patriarch of old, talked and prayed for them, despite chest pains and labored breathing. Nothing would have pleased him more than to have gathered all thirteen of his grandchildren, but they were scattered too far, including Richard's eldest son, M.R. II, who was now a student at Moody Bible Institute in Chicago.

The Doctor rallied from this sinking experience, but afterward expressed some disappointment. "I went through all the death agonies, and I thought sure I would open my eyes and see the Lord," he told a visitor. "I'm so curious I can hardly wait. Now I'll have to go through the death struggle again."

By this time Dr. DeHaan had completed his twenty-ninth, and last, book, *Portraits of Christ in Genesis.* As his strength permitted, he worked at taping these messages in his studio at home. He expressed great concern to members of the family—and to the Lord—that the entire series be aired on the *Radio Bible Class.* Richard assured him that if God should call his father home before he could air the series himself, Richard would complete the series from the manuscript. The Doctor seemed to breathe a sigh of relief upon hearing this. It not only told him that the Genesis lessons would all be broadcast but assured him that Richard would be carrying on the ministry.

❋   ❋   ❋

The alternately gray and bright, crisp December days passed slowly for the Doctor. Propped on a large green chair in his bedroom, his face benign and tired, he watched the ever-changing scene from his window. Ice partially covered the lake formed by the Thornapple River, and occasionally children skated near the shore, perhaps fifty yards away. Birds flitted here and there in search of food, and sometimes a rabbit hopped by, oblivious to the eyes of the pajama-clad figure watching from the bedroom. A light, wet snow during the night turned the outdoors into a lacy white wonderland accented against a blue sky swept clean of clouds by the morning sun. "My Father painted this magnificent scene," the Doctor would say.

On Saturday, December 11, M.R.'s physician prescribed quinine for heart palpitations, and the weary patient took a dose about 4:00 p.m. His son Marvin visited with him, leaving for home on Sunday. Daughter Ruth and Richard's wife, Marge, both nurses, alternated in caring for him, as they had done for the past two weeks. Sunday night he suffered a severe attack, gasping for breath till his complexion seemed almost blue. Oxygen from the tank beside his bed ultimately gave him relief.

Monday morning, December 13, Ruth changed his bedding, sponged him off, and he seemed refreshed enough to attempt another Genesis tape. "Put a chair here and there from my bed to the study, and if I can't make it, I'll sit down and rest." He managed to record almost an entire message before he weakened to the point that Ruth had to help him back to bed.

That afternoon Henry Bosch and Dr. Raymond Brown from the office visited with him for a few minutes. "Why, there's old Caleb!" the Doctor quipped upon seeing the aged, white-haired Dr. Brown. M.R. was in pajamas, raised slightly in the hospital bed that had been obtained for him, his Bible and writing materials at his side. He was preparing meditations for *Our Daily Bread*.

To both visitors, the Doctor seemed stronger than they had expected. Though they did most of the talking, he added gravelly bits of humor to the conversation and told of recording a partial Genesis message that morning. Bosch ended the visit with prayer, and the men returned to the office, much encouraged.

About 4:30 that afternoon, Dr. DeHaan asked his wife for his bathrobe and slippers, and she helped him to the green chair beside his bed. Ruth had gone home, two doors away. Meantime, her husband Tony dropped in, and he and M.R. talked quietly, admiring the icy scene on the lake out back.

At about 5:30, M.R., breathing heavily, asked Tony for the oxygen mask. Before his son-in-law could turn on the oxygen, the beloved teacher gasped and was gone. He had entered the "gates that swing outward never" and was in the presence of the King.

❋　❋　❋

As M.R. himself had once written, nothing compares "with the home-going of a saint of God . . . to go Home, to leave these old clods of clay, to be loosed from bondage of the material, to be set free, to say good-by to mortality . . . welcomed by the innumerable company of angels, and then—glory, hallelujah—to be introduced to the King, and hear Him say, 'Welcome home, my child.' . . . No wonder the Bible says, 'Precious in the sight of the Lord is the death of His saints'" (Psalm 116:15).

In the hours following her husband's death, numerous messages came to Priscilla DeHaan: "A stout oaken timber in God's forest has fallen." . . . "For Dr. DeHaan, a higher calling. For us a great loss." . . . "He was beloved by all of us and will be greatly missed." . . . "He will be remembered over much of the world as valiant for God's truth." . . . "When we told our children, our eight-year-old burst into tears. That's how much Dr. DeHaan and his books and booklets and program have been a part of our lives for the past six years."

The memorial service for Dr. M. R. DeHaan was held at Calvary Undenominational Church, with approximately 1,500 persons coming to pay tribute, including a class member from Montana wearing dust-covered cowboy boots who told someone, "I just had to come . . . to see that man." Dr. Theodore Epp from *Back to the Bible* broadcast and the Rev. Herbert Vander Lugt, Dr. DeHaan's pastor, brought the messages and one of two songs sung by Clair Hess and Ray Felten was the familiar, "Tell Me the Story of Jesus."

Rain that had been falling intermittently for several days had changed to snow during the service. At the gravesite, Dr. Epp, his overcoat collar turned up, prayed and committed the earthly remains of the beloved teacher back to the dust. Somehow the falling snow seemed to symbolize the peace of God that Dr. DeHaan found for himself in Jesus Christ and which he had sought so fervently to bring to his listeners.

The cemetery plot had been hurriedly purchased after M.R.'s death; he never quite believed that he would leave the world by the route of the undertaker. He had often said, though, if he did die, he hoped to be buried near someone who held theological views differing with his concerning the imminent, pretribulation rapture of the church. "Then I can say as we are caught up to be with the Lord, 'I told you so'!" he would quip with his half smile. "But I probably wouldn't really do that, for God says we'll all be changed in the twinkling of an eye."

The simple granite gravestone, guarded by a gnarled, moss-streaked silver maple, eloquently testifies of that great truth that M. R. DeHaan so keenly believed and fervently broadcast around the world:

THE LORD HIMSELF SHALL DESCEND FROM HEAVEN
... AND THE DEAD IN CHRIST SHALL RISE ...
1 THESSALONIANS 4:16

And engraved below that verse:

PERHAPS TODAY

EPILOGUE

In the weeks following his father's death, letters poured in from faithful listeners assuring Richard DeHaan that they were praying for him. Their overwhelming vote of confidence made him realize just how wonderfully Joshua 1:5 was being worked out by God in his life: "As I was with Moses, so I will be with thee: I will not fail thee, nor forsake thee. Be strong and of a good courage."

When M.R. died, the weight of the ministry fell entirely upon Richard's shoulders. The first member of a second generation to carry forward a major religious broadcast—by then heard on nearly six hundred stations around the world—Richard made it clear that the decision to continue was not about family but about the message.

"We look at this as a ministry, rather than the work of a single man," Richard explained in a 1966 newspaper interview following the death of his father. "True, it was my father whom the Lord used to build up the audience, but so many things have happened totally apart from what he was able to do that we believe God wants this radio program to continue."

Richard also ensured that his father's final messages on the book of Genesis made it to the airwaves. He picked up the work where his father left off, studying the lessons he had prepared and then making them his own. Then in 1967, Richard published his own series of lessons titled "The Living God." These were distributed in booklet form to all the class members and were also made available in a clothbound edition.

The changing mantle of leadership was marked by a new outreach. Richard had every intention of continuing and expanding the radio and literature productions, but he also saw that the ministry was in a position to venture into the developing medium of television. In 1968 the first telecast of *Day of Discovery* was aired, having been taped earlier before a live audience in St. Petersburg, Florida.

During Dr. DeHaan's lifetime, as television became popular, his associates remarked on several occasions that the Doctor would be a tremendous TV personality. People liked him on the radio, they reminded him, and liked him even better when they saw and heard him in person.

"I'm not the man for television," he once told Richard. "The Lord gave me radio, and He has blessed it far beyond all I could have dreamed, But, Richard, if you want to go on television, fine!"

The launching of *Day of Discovery* grew out of much prayer and planning on the part of all key RBC personnel. The telecast originated in the Bayfront Center Auditorium in St. Petersburg, Florida, and was broadcast from there for a year before moving to Cypress Gardens, where it was broadcast until the late 1980s. After that, with the advent of portable production equipment, the program could be shot anywhere in the world, as it still is today, with the broadcast headquartered in Grand Rapids.

The innovative *Day of Discovery* television program was well received from the beginning, and with this new venture, additional personnel were needed. Over the next two decades, Radio Bible Class continued to grow both in membership and staff. New additions were made to the offerings, including a family magazine called *Discovery Digest*, and the ministry began taking its first steps toward overseas offices.

In 1985, after leading Radio Bible Class for twenty years, health-related issues, including a diagnosis of Parkinson's disease, led Richard DeHaan to step down from his role as president, passing the baton to the third generation of DeHaans, his son M. R. (Mart) DeHaan II.[1]

Since then RBC has undergone a number of expansions that have extended the arms of the ministry to include the Discovery Series, *Sports Spectrum* magazine, Discovery House Publishers, and in more recent years a significant Internet presence. The expansion also includes such radio broadcasts as *Discover the Word* and *Words to Live By*, and through the years a variety of voices have been heard, including Richard DeHaan, Henry Bosch, Dennis DeHaan, Paul Van Gorder, David Burnham, Billy Strachan, Les Lamborn, Alice Mathews, Haddon Robinson, and Mart DeHaan.

In 1995, in an effort to reflect the broad nature of the ministry's outreach, the leadership decided to change the name from Radio Bible Class to RBC Ministries.

Today, Mart DeHaan and his brother Rick (Richard Jr.) oversee a growing ministry that encompasses almost five hundred paid staff members and many volunteers in thirty-two offices throughout the world. While the ministry in many ways does not resemble the broadcast operation launched by Dr. M. R. DeHaan in 1938, the organization still remains true to his vision of making the life-changing gospel and wisdom of the Bible understandable and accessible to all.

---

1. Richard DeHaan died in 2002. Much of the legacy he left can be summed up in the words of one of his favorite poems: "Trust in God and do the right."

If you visit the RBC headquarters in Grand Rapids, in one corner of the lobby you will find a painting of Dr. M. R. DeHaan, and below it a glass case displaying his Bible, a few pages of his original radio sermon notes, an old microphone and radio, and the "Perhaps Today" plaque that sat on M.R.'s desk. But this is not a shrine. It is simply an acknowledgment and remembrance of how God used the life of one man as he faithfully lived out those closing words of the original *Radio Bible Class* broadcast: "Keep on praying, working, and watching!"

NOTE TO THE READER

The publisher invites you to share your response to the message of this book by writing Discovery House Publishers, PO Box 3566, Grand Rapids, MI 49501, USA. For information about other Discovery House books, music, videos, or DVDs, contact us at the same address or call 1-800-653-8333. Find us on the Internet at http://www.dhp.org/ or send e-mail to books@dhp.org.